EMOTIONAL REGULATION

Mindful Strategies To Enhance Self-Awareness, Build
Resilience, Master Relationships, And Foster Personal
And Professional Growth

BY
TAYLOR YUNG

Table of Contents

WELCOME!

Welcome to Your Journey in Emotional Regulation

Hello, dear reader! Welcome to this journey where you'll explore and learn about emotional regulation—what it is, why it's important, and how you can master it to lead a more balanced and fulfilling life. This book is designed just for you,to help you navigate the sometimes stormy waters ofemotions. Whether you're feeling overwhelmed, frustrated, or just curious about managing your feelings better, you're in the right place.

What is Emotional Regulation?

Emotional regulation is the skill of managing and responding to an emotional experience in a healthy way. It's about notjust controlling your emotions, but understanding and channeling them to work for you, not against you. Think of it like learning to sail a ship; sometimes the sea is calm, and some- times it's incredibly wild. Emotional regulation is the skill of steering your ship no matter the sea conditions.

Why is Emotional Regulation Important?

Imagine you're playing a video game, and you come across a level that's difficult to beat. If you react by throwing the controller or giving up, you won't win the game. But if you stay calm, learn from your mistakes, and try again, your chances of succeeding are much higher.

In real life, being able to manage your emotions effectively can lead to better relationships, improved mental health, and stronger performance at school or work. It's like being the director of your own emotional movie; you get to decidewhat happens next, even if the script takes an unexpected turn.

What Will You Learn?

Through this book, you will find:

- Tools to Understand Your Emotions: Learn whatemotions are, where they come from, and what purpose they serve.
- Strategies for Regulation: We'll explore various techniques to manage intense emotions, from mindfulness to thinking back to restructuring yourthoughts.
- Scenarios: Stories that will help you visualize theprocesses of regulation
- Real-Life Applications: Find out how to apply these strategies in everyday situations, whether it's preparing for a test, handling a conflict, or just managing day-to-day stress.
- Ways for Building Resilience: Learn how to strengthen your emotional stability and resilience, so that managing your feelings becomes easier and more natural.
- Ideas for Resources: Real-life applications forimplementing what you're learning

How to Use This Book

This book is set up to be interactive and practical. Each chapter introduces new ideas and tools, followed by exercisesthat you can do on your own or with friends and family. There's no right or wrong way to go about it—feel free to proceed at your own pace and revisit sections as needed.

You're Not Alone

Remember, everyone struggles with their emotions at times—it's part of being human. By choosing to read this book, you'retaking a brave step toward understanding and mastering your own emotions. So, give yourself credit for this significant move.

We hope you find this book a valuable companion on your path to emotional regulation. Get ready to learn, explore, and transform. Let's embark on this adventure together!

PART ONE

SKILLS FOR DEVELOPING SELF-AWARENESS AND EMOTIONAL REGULATION

INTRODUCTION:
SELF-AWARENESS

Self-awareness is like having a mirror for your mind and emotions, not just your appearance. It means knowing your thoughts, feelings, and habits, and how these elements shape your actions and reactions. Imagine you're the captain of a ship, and self-awareness is your map and compass combined. It helps you understand where you are, where you're headed, and how to navigate through life's waters.

Why is self-awareness so valuable? Well, it's a bit like having a superpower. When you understand your thoughts and feelings, you can make better decisions, improve your relation- ships, and lead a more fulfilling life. It's like being in a video game where you know not just the controls but also the best strategies to win. Self-aware people can recognize when they're feeling upset or happy and why, making it easier to handle stress and enjoy life's good moments. They're like social ninjas, navigating through conversations and interactions with a deeper understanding of themselves and others.

DEFINITION: Emotions and why we want to regulate them.

Emotions are like the weather of the mind, constantly changing and affecting everything we do, think, and say. They are powerful feelings that arise from our experiences, thoughts, and surroundings. They influence our decisions and how we view the world. Just as the weather can vary from sunny to stormy, our emotions can range from joy and love to anger and sadness.

Imagine emotions as the color palette of life. Each emotion adds a unique hue to our experiences, painting our memories with vibrant shades of happiness, sadness, fear, and excitement. These colors make our lives more vivid and meaningful, helping us to appreciate the beauty of our happiest moments and learn from our challenges.

At their core, emotions are signals. They alert us to what's happening around us and within us. For example, fear might be a warning of danger, telling us to be cautious. Joy, on the other hand, could be a sign that we're doing something right, encouraging us to keep going.

Like a compass, emotions guide our actions, nudging us towards what feels right and away from harm.

Emotions are deeply connected to our physical bodies as well. When we're scared, our hearts might race, readying us to flee or fight. When we're happy, we might feel a lightness, an energy that wasn't there before. This connection shows how intertwined our minds and bodies are, each emotion triggering a physical response that prepares us for action.

But emotions aren't just personal. They are also about connection. They help us communicate with others, building relationships and communities. A smile can share our happiness, while tears can express our pain, drawing others to comfort us. Emotions are the language of the human experience, allowing us to understand and support each other on a deep level.

Understanding and managing emotions is a crucial skill. It's slike learning to navigate a ship on the high seas. By recognizing and respecting our emotions, we can steer throughlife's challenges more effectively, making decisions that lead to happiness and well-being. This doesn't mean suppressing our feelings but rather acknowledging them, understanding their origins, and deciding how best to act on them.

In summary, emotions are complex and vital aspects of our human experience. They color our perceptions, guide our decisions, connect us with others, and even affect our physical state. By learning to understand and navigate our emotions, we gain insight into ourselves and the world around us, enhancing our ability to live fulfilling and meaningful lives.

Why do we want to Regulate our Emotions?

Learning to regulate emotions is like learning to drive a car: it gives you control over where you're going and how you get there, even when the road gets bumpy. Emotional regulation isn't about shutting down feelings or pretending they don't exist; it's about understanding them, managing their intensity, and responding to them in a way that's helpful, not harmful.

In essence, learning to regulate emotions is a crucial life skill. It's not about suppressing what you feel but about under- standing and managing your emotions to live a balanced, fulfilling life. Just as driving lessons prepare you for the road, learning emotional regulation prepares you for the journey of life, equipped to handle its twists and turns with confidence and poise.

Now that we have defined Self-Awareness and the value of Emotional Regulation, let's explore skills we can develop to enhance Emotional Regulation for each of us.

RECOGNIZING YOUR EMOTIONS

Recognizing and labeling our emotions accurately is like being the captain of a ship sailing through the sea of feelings. Just as a captain needs to recognize the signs of the weather, we need to understand our emotions to navigate our lives better. This skill is the first step in enhancing self-awareness, which is super important for everyone, especially for young adults like you, who are on the exciting journey of discovering who you are. Let's dive into why this is crucial and how you can master this skill.

UNDERSTANDING EMOTIONS

Emotions are like the waves in the sea; they can be calm and peaceful, but sometimes they can be overwhelming and hard to control. Emotions are a big part of what makes us human. They influence our decisions, how we react to situations, and how we interact with people. But before we can manage these emotions, we first have to recognize and name them. This might sound simple, but it's actually a bit of a challenge.

WHY RECOGNIZING AND LABELING EMOTIONS IS IMPORTANT

Imagine you're feeling really upset about something, but you're not sure why. Maybe you're angry, maybe you're sad, or maybe it's a mix of both. If you don't know exactly how you're feeling, it can be hard to figure out why you feel that way and what you can do about it. Recognizing and labeling your emotions is like having a map and compass while sailing. It helps you understand where you are, so you can decide where to go next.

HOW TO RECOGNIZE AND LABEL YOUR EMOTIONS

Recognizing and labeling your emotions isn't always easy, but with practice, it becomes easier. Here are some steps to help you get started:

- **Pay Attention to Your Feelings:** Sometimes we're so busy with our day-to-day lives that we don't stop to think about how we're feeling. Take a moment to check in with yourself. How are you feeling right now?

- **Notice Physical Signs:** Our bodies often show signs of our emotions before we're fully aware of them. For example, a racing heart might mean you're anxious, or a heavy feeling in your chest might mean you're sad. Paying attention to these signs can help you recognize your emotions.

- **Name the Emotion:** Once you've noticed how you're feeling, try to put a name to it. Are you feeling happy, sad, angry, frustrated, excited? Sometimes, you might feel a mix of emotions, and that's okay too.
- **Practice Makes Perfect:** Like any skill, recognizing and labeling your emotions takes practice. You won't be perfect at it overnight, but the more you do it, the better you'll get.

WHY IT CAN BE HARD

Recognizing and labeling emotions can be tricky for a few reasons.

First: we're not always taught to pay attention to our emotions. We might be told to "toughen up" or that showing emotions is a sign of weakness, which isn't true at all. Emotions are a normal part of being human, and recognizing them is a sign of strength, not weakness.

Second: sometimes we might feel ashamed or scared of our emotions, especially if they're considered negative, like anger or sadness. It's important to remember that all emotions are valid. They're indicators of what's happening inside us and can teach us a lot about ourselves.

Finally: emotions can be complex and confusing. Sometimes, what we feel doesn't fit neatly into one category. You might feel a blend of emotions at the same time, making it harder to label them accurately. But with practice, you'll get better at understanding your emotional landscape.

Let's explore a hypothetical scenario where a young adult, named Jordan, learns to enhance emotional regulation by recognizing his emotions.

Scenario: Jordan's Path to Recognizing Emotions

Before: Jordan, a college freshman, often found himself reacting impulsively in stressful situations. Whether it was snapping at a roommate for a minor inconvenience or feeling overwhelmed by coursework deadlines, Jordan's emotions seemed to control him more than he controlled them. After a particularly intense outburst over a misplaced textbook, Jordan realized this pattern of reacting rather than responding was damaging his relationships and his mental health.

The Turning Point: Jordan's sociology professor introduced the class to the concept of emotional intelligence, emphasizing the importance of recognizing one's emotions as the first step toward managing them effectively. Inspired, Jordan decided to focus on identifying his feelings as they occurred, hoping to understand his emotional triggers better.

Practicing Awareness: Jordan began by keeping a simple journal. Every evening, he would reflect on moments whenhe felt strong emotions throughout the day, noting what thosefeelings were, what he thought triggered them, and how he reacted. This practice wasn't about judging his reactions but rather observing them.

A Common Scenario: One day, Jordan felt a wave of frustration when he couldn't grasp a concept during his math study session. Instead of his usual response of pushing the books away and giving up, he paused. Jordan acknowledged he wasfeeling frustrated and overwhelmed. Recognizing these emotions allowed him to address them directly—he took a deep breath, reminded himself that it's okay to find topics challenging, and decided to take a short break before trying again with a clearer mind.

Seeking Constructive Solutions: With time, Jordan noticed patterns in his emotional responses. He identified that feeling unprepared or behind on coursework was a significant trigger for his stress and frustration. With this insight, Jordan began to proactively manage his schedule better, dedicating specific times for studying and starting assignments well before their due dates.

Improvement in Relationships: Recognizing his emotions also improved Jordan's interactions with others. When he felt annoyed or irritated with his roommate, he would acknowledge the feeling and consider why he felt that way before speaking. This led to more constructive conversations and less conflict. Jordan explained this new approach to his room-mate, who appreciated the effort and reciprocated by being more open about his own feelings.

Outcome: Over the semester, Jordan noticed a significant shift in how he managed his emotions. By recognizing and acknowledging his feelings, he could choose how to respond rather than react impulsively. This not only reduced the frequency of his stress-induced outbursts but also improved his relationships and academic performance.

Conclusion: Jordan's journey highlights the transformative power of recognizing one's emotions. Through self-reflection and practice, Jordan learned to identify his feelings and understand their triggers, which allowed him to develop healthier coping mechanisms and improve his emotional regulation. This process helped Jordan navigate the challenges of college life with greater resilience and emotional intelligence, illustrating that understanding our emotions is the first step toward mastering them.

TIPS FOR GETTING BETTER AT THIS SKILL

- **Use a Feelings Chart:** Sometimes, having a list of emotions in front of you can help you identify what you're feeling. There are many feelings charts available online that you can use as a reference.

- **Talk About Your Feelings:** Sharing how you feel with someone you trust can help you clarify your emotions. Sometimes, just talking about it out loud can help you understand and label your feelings better.

- **Write It Down:** Keeping a journal of your emotions can be very helpful. When you write down how you feel, you're forced to think about it more deeply, helping you to recognize and label your emotions accurately. We will explore this more in a bit.

- **Read Books or Watch Movies:** Books and movies are great for exploring a range of emotions. Pay attention to how characters are feeling and why. This can help you become more aware of your own emotions and give you the words to describe them.

APPLYING THIS SKILL IN REAL LIFE

Recognizing and labeling your emotions is more than just a

personal exercise; it's a tool that can improve your interactions with others. When you understand how you're feeling, you can communicate more clearly, avoid misunderstandings, and build stronger relationships. It can also help you make better decisions. Instead of reacting impulsively based on how you feel in the moment, you can recognize your emotions and decide the best way to respond.

Conclusion

Recognizing and labeling your emotions is the first step towards self-awareness and emotional regulation. It's like learning to read the compass and map of your inner world. This skill will not only help you navigate your own emotions but also improve your relationships and decision-making. Remember, it's okay to feel a wide range of emotions, and practicing how to identify and express them is a journey worth taking. So, next time you feel something stirring inside, take a moment to pause, recognize it, give it a name, and remember: understanding your emotions is the key to mastering them.

Prompts for Successful Journaling

Getting started can be the hardest part of journaling. Each time you sit down to journal, select one of the prompts below. Read the questions, and reflect as you write your thoughts in your journal. Once you start, the only thing that follows is goodness and awareness.

Here are 20 journaling prompts tailored for young adults focusing on emotional regulation. These prompts are designed to explore feelings, thoughts, and reactions, helping to foster self-awareness and emotional growth.

- **Reflect on a Recent Challenge:** Think of a recent situation that was challenging for you emotionally. What happened, and how did you feel at that moment? How did you respond, and what would you do differently next time?

- **Identify Your Triggers:** Write about things or situations that trigger strong emotions in you. Why do you think these triggers affect you the way they do?

- **Explore Your Joy:** What activities or moments make you feel genuinely happy and at peace? Describe how you can incorporate more of these moments into your daily life.

- **Dealing with Anger:** Think of a time when you felt angry. What caused it, and how did you express your anger? Reflect on constructive ways to deal with anger when it arises.

- **Understanding Sadness:** Write about what sadness feels like to you. Can you pinpoint what usually causes your sadness? How do you cope with these feelings?

- **Confront a Fear:** Describe a fear you have and why it scares you. How does this fear affect your life, and what steps could you take to face it?

- **Self-Compassion Exercise:** Write a letter to yourself from the perspective of a kind and understanding friend. What would this friend say to you about yourrecent struggles?

- **Your Achievements:** Reflect on your accomplishments and what you are proud of. How did you overcome the obstacles to reach your goals?

- **Gratitude List:** Make a list of things you are gratefulfor in your life. How do these things impact your mood and overall outlook?

- **The Role of Friendship:** Think about your relationships with friends. How do they influence your emotional well-being? Are there friendships youneed to re-evaluate?

- **When You Feel Overwhelmed:** Describe a situationwhen you felt overwhelmed by emotions. What coping strategies helped you manage these feelings?

- **Learning from Mistakes:** Reflect on a mistake and what you learned from it. How has this experience helped you grow?

- **Setting Boundaries:** Write about a time you had to set boundaries for your emotional health. Why was it necessary, and how did you feel afterward?

- **Dreams and Aspirations:** What are your dreams forthe future? How do these aspirations reflect your values and desires?

- **Facing Disappointment:** Think about a time you faced disappointment. How did you deal with it, and what did it teach you about expectations and reality?

- **The Influence of Social Media:** Reflect on how social media affects your emotions. Are there changes you could make to your social media habits for better emotional health?

- **Your Support System:** Who do you turn to when you need support? Describe how these individuals help you through tough times.

- **Managing Stress:** Identify what stresses you out and how you usually manage stress. Are there more effective strategies you could try?

- **Embracing Change:** Write about a change you're currently experiencing or one that's upcoming. How do you feel about it, and how can you prepare emotionally?

- **Self-Identity and Growth:** Reflect on how you've changed over the past year. What have been the significant drivers of this change, and how do you feel about the person you're becoming?

These prompts are intended to encourage introspection and emotional growth. Journaling can be a powerful tool for understanding and regulating your emotions, leading to a healthier and more balanced life.

REFLECTIONS

CULTIVATING SELF-COMPASSION

Cultivating self-compassion is like becoming your own best friend, offering support and understanding to yourself, especially during tough times. This approach to treating yourself can significantly help with emotional regulation, making it easier to manage feelings like sadness, anger, or frustration. Here's why and how:

WHY CULTIVATING SELF-COMPASSION HELPS WITH EMOTIONAL REGULATION:

- **Reduces Self-Criticism:** Often, we are our own harshest critics. Imagine if every time you stumbled, someone yelled at you instead of offering a hand. That's what self-criticism does; it makes you feel worse. Self-compassion quietens this inner critic, reducing stress and making it easier to navigate emotional ups and downs.

- **Encourages a Balanced Perspective:** Self-compassion helps you see your experiences as part of the human condition everyone has tough times. This perspective is like stepping back to see the whole forest, not just the tree you bumped into. It allowsyou to treat your feelings with kindness, understanding they're normal and manageable.

- **Boosts Resilience:** Being kind to yourself, especially when things don't go as planned, builds resilience. It'slike putting on armor; it doesn't make the challenges disappear, but it helps you face them without getting as hurt. This resilience is key to bouncing back from setbacks and managing emotional reactions.

Let's explore a hypothetical scenario involving a young adult named Sofia, who discovers how cultivating self-compassion significantly improves her emotional regulation.

Scenario: Sofia's Journey to Self-Compassion

Before: Sofia, a 20-year-old college student, often found herself caught in a cycle of self-criticism and perfectionism. Whether it was a grade that didn't meet her high standards ora social interaction that didn't go as planned, Sofia would berate herself for days. This constant internal criticism led to heightened stress and moments of intense emotional turmoil, making it difficult for her to bounce back from even minor setbacks.

The Turning Point: After a particularly tough week where nothing seemed to go right, Sofia confided in her aunt, a ther-apist, who introduced her to the concept of self-compassion. Her aunt explained that being kind to oneself in moments of failure or difficulty could lead to greater emotional resilience. Intrigued, Sofia decided to learn more about how she could be more compassionate towards herself.

Practicing Self-Compassion: Sofia started by identifying moments when she was being overly critical of herself. Instead of spiraling into self-criticism after receiving a B on a paper, she paused and acknowledged the effort she had put into her work. She told herself what she would tell a friend in a similar situation: "You worked hard, and a B is a good grade. This doesn't define your intelligence or worth."

Cultivating Mindfulness: Sofia realized that acknowledging her feelings without judgment was crucial for self-compassion. She began practicing mindfulness, focusing on accepting her emotions as they were. When feelings of inadequacy arose, she would gently remind herself, "It's okay to feel this way. Let's breathe through it."

Common Kindness: Sofia made an effort to treat herself as kindly as she would treat a friend. She put together a self-care kit filled with things that made her feel comforted and calm, like her favorite tea, a cozy blanket, and a journal. Whenever she felt overwhelmed, she would turn to her kit, reminding herself that it was okay to take breaks and care for her well- being.

Challenging Negative Self-Talk: Sofia also worked on changing the way she spoke to herself. Every time she caught herself slipping into negative self-talk, she would stop and reframe her thoughts in a more compassionate and under- standing way. For example, instead of thinking, "I'm such a failure," she'd remind herself, "Everyone makes mistakes. What can I learn from this?"

The Outcome: Over time, Sofia noticed a significant shift in how she responded to stress and setbacks. By treating herself with kindness and understanding, she found that she could navigate difficult emotions more calmly and recover from disappointments more quickly. This newfound self-compas- sion didn't just lower her stress levels; it also improved her relationships, as she became less defensive and more open to feedback.

Conclusion: Sofia's journey demonstrates the profound impact of self-compassion on emotional regulation. By learning to be kind and understanding toward herself, Sofia developed the resilience to face life's challenges without being overwhelmed by negative emotions. This story high- lights that the journey to emotional regulation begins with how we treat ourselves in our most vulnerable moments. Through self-compassion, we can cultivate a stronger, more forgiving relationship with ourselves, leading to a healthier emotional life.

SKILLS TO BUILD MORE SELF-COMPASSION:

- **Mindfulness:** Mindfulness is about being present in the moment without judgment. When you're mindful, you observe your thoughts and feelings as they are, without labeling them as good or bad. It's like watching clouds pass in the sky; you notice them but don't get swept away. This awareness can help you respond to your emotions with compassion instead of criticism.

- **Self-Kindness:** Treat yourself as you would a good friend. When you're struggling, ask yourself, "What would I say to a friend in this situation?" Then, direct those kind words and actions toward yourself. This could be taking a break, offering words of encouragement, or simply acknowledging that it's okay to be imperfect.

- **Common Humanity:** Recognize that suffering and personal shortcomings are part of the shared human experience. Instead of feeling isolated in your struggles, remind yourself that you're not alone.

- Others have been here too. This connection can make your own challenges feel more bearable and less personal.

- **Gratitude Journaling:** Writing down things you're grateful for, including aspects about yourself, can shift your focus from criticism to appreciation. It's like making a highlight reel of your positive qualities and experiences, which can foster a more compassionate self-view.

- **Self-Compassion Breaks:** Whenever you notice you're

feeling stressed or critical towards yourself, take a brief pause. Close your eyes, place a hand over your heart, and offer yourself some comforting words or simply acknowledge your feelings. This break is like hitting the reset button, giving you a chance to approach the situation with kindness.

By cultivating self-compassion, you equip yourself with a supportive and understanding ally yourself. This ally can help navigate the emotional landscapes of life with more ease, promoting a healthier, more balanced emotional state. Like any skill, it takes practice, but the benefits to your emotional well-being and overall happiness are well worth the effort.

REFLECTIONS

UNDERSTANDING TRIGGERS

After learning how to recognize and label your emotions, the next step in boosting your self-awareness journey is understanding your triggers.

Triggers are like the buttons on a video game controller; when pressed, they cause a reaction. In real life, these triggers can be situations, words, people, or even smells that spark a certain emotion in you. Understanding what sets off these emotions is crucial because it helps you manage how you respond. Let's dive deeper into this step and see how you can become a trigger detective in your own life.

WHAT ARE TRIGGERS?

Imagine you're walking down the street, and you see a dog that looks just like one that bit you when you were younger. Suddenly, you feel scared, even though this dog isn't doing anything scary. That's a trigger. The sight of the dog brings back feelings of fear because of your past experience. Triggers can be anything. Maybe a certain song makes you feel sad because it reminds you of a sad time in your life. Or perhaps the smell of a certain food makes you happy because it reminds you of fun family gatherings.

WHY UNDERSTANDING TRIGGERS IS IMPORTANT

Understanding your triggers is like having a map of a mine-field. If you know where the mines (or triggers) are, you can navigate around them more safely. This doesn't mean you'll never get upset or have strong emotions, but it does mean you'll be better prepared to deal with them when they come up. For example, if you know that you get really angry when you're hungry (sometimes called being "hangry"), you can make sure to carry a snack with you. This way, you can avoid getting too hungry and becoming easily angered.

HOW TO RECOGNIZE YOUR TRIGGERS

Recognizing your triggers requires you to be a bit of a detective. Here are some steps to help you start uncovering your triggers:

- **Keep an Emotions Journal:** Just like when you were learning to recognize and label your emotions, keeping a journal can help with identifying triggers. Write down when you feel strong emotions and what was happening around that time. Look for patterns over time.

- **Ask Why:** When you feel a strong emotion, ask yourself why you're feeling this way. Can you connect it to something specific that happened? This can help you start to see what your triggers are.

- **Think About Your Past:** Sometimes, our triggers are connected to past experiences. If something in your past was upsetting or traumatic, similar situations in the present might trigger those same feelings.

- **Notice Your Physical Reactions:** Just like emotions can have physical signs, so can triggers. Maybe your heart races or you start to sweat. Noticing these signs can help you recognize when you're being triggered.

TIPS FOR MANAGING YOUR TRIGGERS

Once you've started to identify some of your triggers, the next step is learning how to manage them. Here are some strategies:

- **Plan Ahead:** If you know certain situations trigger you, plan for how you can handle them. If big crowds make you anxious, and you have to go to a crowded place, think about ways to stay calm ahead of time.

- **Use Calming Techniques:** Breathing exercises, mindfulness, and other calming techniques can help you manage your reactions when you're faced with a trigger.

- **Communicate with Others:** If certain words or actions from people are triggers for you, it might be helpful to let them know calmly and clearly. They may not realize what they're doing is affecting you.

- **Seek Support:** Sometimes, we need help from others to manage our triggers, especially if they're related to something traumatic from our past. Talking to a trusted adult, counselor, or therapist can be really helpful.

WHAT PART DOES NUTRITION PLAY IN UNDERSTANDING TRIGGERS?

The path to emotional awareness and regulation is not just about understanding your triggers but also about nurturing your body and mind with the right nutritional building blocks. Here are some key reminders:

The Brain-Gut Connection

Firstly, it's important to understand the connection between your brain and your gut, often referred to as the "second brain." This is not just because it helps us make decisions about what to eat, but because there is a communication highway between the gut and the brain, known as the vagus nerve. Imagine this nerve as a two-way radio, constantly sending messages back and forth. When you eat nutritious foods, it's like sending positive, calming messages along this highway, which can help in managing emotions more effectively. On the flip side, poor nutrition can send distress signals, making it harder to deal with emotional triggers.

Nutrients and Neurotransmitters

Think of neurotransmitters as messengers in your brain that influence your feelings and emotions. Serotonin, for example, is a neurotransmitter that helps regulate mood, and it's largely produced in the gut. Foods rich in tryptophan (like turkey, eggs, and cheese) are key ingredients for producing serotonin. It's like adding a scoop of happiness to your brain's chemical recipe. Similarly, omega-3 fatty acids found in fish, flaxseeds, and walnuts are like lubricants for your brain, helping improve communication between brain cells, which can make it easier to recognize and manage emotional triggers.

Blood Sugar Levels

The story doesn't end there. Imagine your energy levels and mood as a rollercoaster. What you eat can either make this ride smooth or full of sudden drops. Consuming a lot of simple carbohydrates and sugary foods can cause spikes in your blood sugar levels, followed by rapid drops. This roller- coaster can lead to mood swings, making emotional triggers more difficult to handle. Instead, incorporating complex carbohydrates like whole grains, fruits, and vegetables can help maintain steady blood sugar levels, making the emotional ride smoother and more manageable.

Inflammatory Foods

Lastly, some foods cause inflammation in the body, which can affect the brain and mood. Think of inflammation as a silent alarm system that, when constantly triggered by unhealthy food choices (like too much processed food, sugar, and trans fats), can make the brain more susceptible to emotional stress.By choosing anti-inflammatory foods like berries, leafygreens, and nuts, you're essentially turning off unnecessary alarm bells, reducing stress, and improving your ability to cope with emotional triggers.

Conclusion

In summary, just like a garden that flourishes with the right care and nutrients, your emotional well-being can signifi- cantly benefit from proper nutrition. By becoming aware of the food-mood connection, you can better understand and manage your emotional triggers. This doesn't mean you need to overhaul your diet overnight. Instead, consider making small, mindful changes, like incorporating more whole foods and staying hydrated, to support your emotional regulation journey.

UNDERSTANDING TRIGGERS IN RELATIONSHIPS

Triggers can play a big role in how we interact with others.

For example, if you're triggered by feeling ignored and your friend doesn't text you back right away, you might feel upset or angry. But if you understand this trigger, you can remind yourself that just because your friend hasn't responded yet doesn't mean they're ignoring you. Recognizing and managing your triggers can help prevent misunderstandings and strengthen your relationships.

Let's dive into a couple of hypothetical scenarios that showcase how young adults can boost their emotional regulation by getting to know their triggers better. Understanding what sets off certain emotions can help manage reactions and makemore mindful choices.

Scenario 1: Marcus and the Group Project

Before Understanding Triggers: Marcus used to get really frustrated during group projects, especially when he felt his ideas weren't being heard. This frustration often led to him shutting down or snapping at his group mates, which didn't help the project or his relationships with classmates.

Identifying the Trigger: After one particularly tense group meeting, Marcus took some time to reflect on why he was feeling so upset. He realized that his frustration spiked when- ever he felt ignored, stemming from a fear that his contributions weren't valued. Recognizing this trigger was a lightbulb moment for Marcus.

Strategy for Emotional Regulation: Marcus decided to try a new approach for the next group project. Before the meeting, he practiced how to assertively express his ideas and also prepared himself mentally for the possibility of his suggestions not being chosen every time. He reminded himself that everyone's ideas deserved space, and not being picked didn't mean his ideas were bad.

After: "Understanding my trigger has really changed how I approach group work," Marcus reflects. "Now, I feel calmer during our discussions. I've learned to express my ideas confidently and to listen to others more openly. Our last project was the best yet, and I even enjoyed the process. It feels great to work as a real team."

Scenario 2: Zoe and Social Media

Before Understanding Triggers: Zoe found herself feeling really down after scrolling through social media. She couldn't pinpoint why, but it made her hesitant to even check her accounts, missing out on connecting with friends online.

Identifying the Trigger: Zoe decided to pay more attention to her feelings during her social media use to figure out what exactly was making her feel so bad. She noticed that posts about extravagant vacations or perfect relationships were the main culprits, triggering feelings of inadequacy and jealousy.

Strategy for Emotional Regulation: With this insight, Zoe made a conscious choice to curate her social media feed. She unfollowed accounts that made her feel bad about herself and started following more that inspired her or made her laugh. She also set limits on her daily social media use to give herself time to engage in activities that might boost her mood, like drawing or biking.

After: "I never realized how much impact social media had on my emotions until I figured out my triggers," says Zoe. "Now, my feed is a much happier place for me, filled with positivity and inspiration. I feel better about myself and enjoy my real-life experiences more. It's like I've taken back control of my happiness."

These scenarios illustrate the power of understanding andaddressing emotional triggers. By recognizing what sets off negative feelings, both Marcus and Zoe were able to devise strategies that improved their emotional regulation, leading to better outcomes in group dynamics and personal well-being.

Understanding your triggers is a crucial step in enhancing your self-awareness and managing your emotions effectively.It requires you to pay close attention to your feelings, reactions, and the situations that cause them. Remember, it's a process that takes time and practice. But as you become more aware of your triggers, you'll be better equipped to navigate your emotional world. You'll be able to approach situations with a clearer mind and make choices that lead to healthier and happier outcomes. So, grab your detective hat and start uncovering the clues to your triggers. Your journey to self-awareness and emotional mastery is well underway!

REFLECTIONS

REFLECTIVE PRACTICES OR THINKING BACK

Developing reflective practices, or what we can call "thinking back," is like turning on a flashlight in a dark room. Suddenly, you can see everything more clearly—the good stuff, the not-so-good stuff, and everything in between. This third step in enhancing self-awareness is all about learning to understand yourself better by reflecting on your experiences, feelings, and actions. It's like being a detective in your own life, investigating to find out more about who you are and how you can grow. Let's explore why "thinking back" is so important and how you can get better at it.

UNDERSTANDING "THINKING BACK"

"Thinking back" means taking time to review your day, your reactions to different situations, and how you felt about them. It's asking yourself why you felt a certain way when your friend said something unexpected or why you got so frustrated with your homework. This kind of self-reflection helps you understand your emotions and actions better.

WHY IS "THINKING BACK" IMPORTANT?

- **Know Yourself Better:** The more you think back, the better you understand your likes, dislikes, strengths, and areas where you can improve. It's like knowing your favorite game inside and out, which helps you play it better.

- **Learn From Experiences:** Every day is full of lessons, but unless you think back on what happened, you might miss them. Reflecting helps you learn from both the wins and the losses.

- **Handle Emotions Smarter:** By understanding your feelings through reflection, you can find better ways to deal with tough situations instead of just reacting on the spot.

- **Make Better Decisions:** When you think back on the choices you've made and their outcomes, you start to see patterns. This insight can help you make smarter decisions in the future.

Let's dive into a hypothetical scenario involving a young adult named Theo, who discovers the power of "thinking back" skills to enhance his emotional regulation.

Scenario: Theo's Mastery of "Thinking Back" for Emotional Regulation

Before: Theo, a 22-year-old recent college graduate, often found himself reacting impulsively to stressful situations, especially at his new job. Feedback from his boss, tight dead-lines, and even small misunderstandings with coworkers would quickly escalate his stress levels, leading to anxiety and occasional outbursts of frustration. Theo realized these reactions were not only harming his professional reputation but also affecting his mental health.

The Turning Point: After a particularly tense meeting where Theo's reaction was more intense than warranted, a close colleague suggested he might benefit from reflecting on his reactions to understand them better. Intrigued by this idea, Theo started researching and learned about the "thinking back" technique as a way to enhance emotional regulation.

Developing "Thinking Back" Skills: Theo began by dedicating a few minutes at the end of each day to reflect on instances when he felt particularly emotional at work. He focused on identifying what triggered these emotions and how he responded. He asked himself questions like, "What exactly upset me about that interaction?" and "Could I have interpreted the situation differently?"

A Common Scenario: One day, Theo felt a surge of anger when his boss pointed out a mistake in his report during a team meeting. Using his "thinking back" skills, Theo later reflected on why this had upset him so much. He realized that he was interpreting constructive feedback as a personal attack on his competence. This insight was a revelation for Theo, who hadn't recognized his sensitivity to criticism before.

Practicing Alternative Responses: With this new understanding, Theo began mentally rehearsing how he could handle similar situations differently in the future. He thought about acknowledging the feedback calmly and viewing it as an opportunity to learn rather than a critique of his worth. He also considered asking for clarification on how to improve, turning the situation into a constructive dialogue.

Seeking External Perspectives: To deepen his reflections, Theo occasionally discussed his "thinking back" insights with trusted friends or family members. These conversations offered additional perspectives that Theo hadn't considered, further aiding his emotional regulation efforts.

The Outcome: Over time, Theo noticed a significant improve-ment in his emotional regulation. By "thinking back" and understanding his triggers and reactions, he learned to pause and choose how to respond rather than being swept up by hisinitial emotions. This not only reduced his stress but alsoimproved his relationships at work. His boss and colleagues began to see him as more composed and receptive to feed- back, which opened the door to more opportunities and responsibilities.

Conclusion: Theo's story illustrates the transformative impact of developing "thinking back" skills on emotional regulation. By reflecting on his emotional responses, under- standing his triggers, and considering alternative ways to react, Theo was able to take control of his emotions rather than letting them control him. This approach not only enhanced his professional life but also contributed to his overall well-being, showcasing the profound benefits of introspection and self-awareness in managing emotions.

HOW TO DEVELOP "THINKING BACK" PRACTICES

Developing a habit of thinking back doesn't require any special tools—just some time and honesty. Here are some ways to get started:

1. Keep a Journal

Writing in a journal is one of the best ways to practice thinking back. At the end of each day, write down what happened, how you felt, and why you think you felt that way. Don't worry about spelling or grammar; this is just for you.

2. Ask Yourself Questions

Questions can guide your reflection. Try asking yourself:

- What made me happy today?
- What did I learn today?
- How did I help someone today?
- What could I have done differently today?

3. Set Aside Quiet Time

Find a quiet spot where you can sit and think about your day without distractions. Even just 10 minutes before bed can be a great time for reflection.

4. Talk It Out

Sometimes, talking about your day with a family member or friend can help you see things from another perspective. Just be sure to choose someone who listens well and respects your feelings.

5. Use Prompts

If you're not sure what to write or think about, you can use prompts. A prompt can be a question or a statement like "The happiest moment of my day was..." or "Something I struggled with today was…"

BENEFITS OF "THINKING BACK"

Understand Your Emotions

"Thinking back" helps you get to the root of your feelings. You might discover that you're not just mad at your sibling for borrowing your stuff without asking but actually feeling upset because you feel your space isn't respected.

Improve Relationships

By reflecting on your interactions with others, you can under-stand how your words and actions affect them. This under- standing can help you communicate better and strengthen your relationships.

Boost Confidence

As you reflect on your achievements and the challenges you've overcome, you'll start to see just how capable you are. This can give you a big confidence boost.

Make Positive Changes

"Thinking back" can highlight habits or behaviors you wantto change. Maybe you notice you're spending too much time on video games and not enough on homework, or you're not standing up for yourself in certain situations. With these insights, you can start to make changes.

CHALLENGES OF "THINKING BACK"

While thinking back is a powerful tool, it can sometimes be tough. You might not always like what you see, or you might find it hard to be honest with yourself about your feelingsand actions. That's okay. The goal isn't to judge yourself harshly but to learn and grow. Be patient and kind to yourselfas you develop this skill.

Conclusion

Developing the practice of thinking back is a journey worth taking. It's a tool that can help you navigate the complexworld of emotions, relationships, and personal growth. By taking the time to reflect on your experiences, you can learnso much about who you are and how you can become even better. Remember, the goal isn't to be perfect but to under- stand yourself better with each passing day. So, grab a jour- nal, find a quiet corner, and start your adventure in thinking back today. Who knows what amazing discoveries lie ahead?

REFLECTIONS

MINDFULNESS AND MEDITATION

WHAT IS MINDFULNESS?

indfulness is paying full attention to whatever you're doing, feeling, or thinking at the moment, without judgment. It's about noticing the small details of your life, whether you're eating, walking, or even breathing. It's the practice of being fully engaged with the present, not lost in thoughts about the past or future.

WHY PRACTICE MINDFULNESS?

- **Reduces Stress:** By focusing on the present, mindfulness reduces stress. It helps you take a break from worrying about things you can't change or predict.

- **Improves Concentration:** Mindfulness trains your brain to focus better. Like a muscle that gets stronger with exercise, your concentration improves the more you practice mindfulness.

- **Enhances Emotional Regulation:** When you're more aware of your thoughts and feelings, you can manage them better. Mindfulness helps you recognize your emotions without getting overwhelmed by them.

- **Increases Empathy and Understanding:** Paying attention to your own thoughts and feelings helps you understand what others might be going through. This can make you more empathetic and improve your relationships.

EASY-TO-FOLLOW MINDFULNESS PRACTICES TAILORED FOR A YOUNG ADULT:

1. Breathing Exercises

One of the simplest yet most powerful mindfulness practices is focusing on your breath. It's like hitting the pause button on a video game, allowing you to take a break from whatever's happening around you.

Practice: Sit comfortably or lie down. Close your eyes and take slow, deep breaths. Inhale through your nose, feeling your stomach rise, and exhale through your mouth, feeling it fall. Focus solely on the sensation of breathing. If your mind wanders, gently bring your attention back to your breath.

2. Body Scan Meditation

This practice is about tuning into your body, noticing how each part feels, without trying to change anything. It's like doing a system check on a computer to see what's running in the background.

Practice: Lie down or sit in a comfortable chair. Close your eyes and start focusing on your toes. Notice any sensations, then gradually move your attention up through your body - your feet, legs, torso, arms, and head. If you notice any tension, don't try to change it; just observe.

3. Mindful Walking

Walking is something you probably do every day without thinking much about it. Turning it into a mindfulness practicecan transform a simple activity into a powerful tool for calming your mind.

Practice: Find a quiet place to walk, like a park or a less busy sidewalk. As you walk, concentrate on the sensation of your feet touching the ground, the rhythm of your steps, and the feel of the air on your skin. If your mind starts to wander, bring your focus back to the act of walking.

4. Mindful Eating

Eating mindfully is about experiencing food more intensely and enjoying the moment without distractions. It's like watching your favorite movie scene by scene, savoring every detail.

Practice: Choose a small snack, like a piece of fruit. Beforeyou eat, look at it closely, noticing its colors, textures, and smells. Take a small bite and chew slowly, focusing on the taste and texture. Try to eat without distractions like TV or your phone.

5. Five Senses Exercise

This practice helps bring your attention to the present by using your five senses. It's a quick way to ground yourself when feeling overwhelmed, like finding a calm spot in the middle of a storm.

Practice: Take a moment to notice five things you can see, four things you can touch, three things you can hear, two things you can smell, and one thing you can taste. This can help redirect your focus from worrying thoughts to the present moment.

Conclusion

Incorporating these mindfulness practices into your daily routine can help improve your emotional regulation. Think of mindfulness as a tool kit; just like you might choose a hammer for a nail or a screwdriver for a screw, you can pick the practice that best suits what you need at the moment. Remember, the key to mindfulness is regular practice. The more you do it, the easier it becomes to tap into that calm, centered feeling, even when emotions run high.

DEVELOPING MINDFULNESS THROUGH MEDITATION

Meditation is one way to practice mindfulness. It's like sitting down for a quiet chat with your mind.

Here's how to get started:

1. **Find a Quiet Spot**

Look for a place where you won't be disturbed. It could be your room, a corner of your living room, or even a spot in your backyard.

2. **Get Comfortable**

Sit or lie down in a comfortable position. You don't have to twist yourself into a pretzel. The goal is to be comfortable enough to focus but not so comfortable that you fall asleep.

3. **Focus on Your Breath**

Close your eyes and pay attention to your breath. Notice how it feels as you breathe in and out. If your mind starts to wander (and it will), gently bring your attention back to your breath.

4. **Start with Short Sessions**

Begin with 5-10 minutes of meditation and gradually increase the time as you get more comfortable with the practice. It's better to have five minutes of focused meditation than 30 minutes of frustration.

OTHER MINDFULNESS PRACTICES

Mindfulness doesn't just happen when you're sitting still. You can practice it throughout your day:

- **Mindful Eating:** Pay attention to the taste, texture, and smell of your food. Eat slowly, and appreciate each bite.
- **Mindful Walking:** Focus on how it feels to walk. Notice the sensation in your feet as they touch the ground, the sounds around you, and the air on your skin.
- **Mindful Listening:** When someone is talking to you, really listen. Notice their words, tone, and how you feel as they speak.

CHALLENGES AND TIPS

Practicing mindfulness and meditation isn't always easy. Your mind will wander, and that's okay. The important thing is to notice when it happens and gently bring your focus back. Don't get frustrated with yourself—remember, it's a practice, not a perfection.

- **Use Apps or Online Guides:** There are many apps and online resources that offer guided meditations and mindfulness exercises.
- **Be Consistent:** Try to make mindfulness and meditation a regular part of your routine, just like brushing your teeth.
- **Be Patient:** Developing mindfulness takes time. Celebrate your progress, no matter how small.

Scenario: Maya's Journey to Emotional Regulation Through Mindfulness and Meditation

Background:

Maya, a 25-year-old software developer, has always prided herself on her ability to manage multiple projects and meet tight deadlines. However, the stress from her fast-paced job has started to affect her mental health. Lately, she finds herself overwhelmed by minor setbacks and snapping at colleagues over trivial issues. Realizing the impact of her emotional volatility, Maya decides to explore mindfulnessand meditation to regain her emotional balance.

Starting the Journey:

It's a typical busy Wednesday afternoon when Maya experiences a surge of anxiety triggered by an upcoming product launch. Remembering the mindfulness techniques she read about, she decides to take a 10-minute break from her desk. Finding a quiet spot in the office garden, Maya sits down, closes her eyes, and begins focusing on her breathing. She usesa simple meditation technique of counting her breaths up to ten and then starting back at one whenever her mind wanders.

Regular Practice:

Encouraged by the initial sense of calm from her first session, Maya commits to regular practice. She starts her mornings with a 15-minute meditation using an app that guides her through different techniques aimed at fostering mindfulness. The app tracks her progress, provides tips on maintaining focus, and explores a variety of meditation styles to keep her engaged.

Challenges and Adaptations:

Despite her best intentions, Maya faces challenges. There are days when she can't seem to focus, and her mind is crowded with thoughts about her work. During these moments, she feels frustrated and considers giving up. However, recalling advice from a podcast on mindfulness, she adopts a non-judgmental attitude towards her wandering thoughts and learns to gently guide her focus back to her breathing without self-criticism.

Applying Mindfulness at Work:

Two months into her mindfulness journey, Maya starts to notice a shift in her reactions at work. During a particularly tense meeting where technical issues are causing delays, she feels her irritation rising. This time, however, she recognizes the onset of her emotional response. Silently, she focuses on her breath, grounding herself in the present moment. This quick mindfulness exercise helps her respond to the situation with composure and provide constructive solutions rather than reacting with frustration.

Broader Impacts:

Maya's commitment to mindfulness visibly reduces her stress levels and improves her interactions with colleagues. Her ability to manage her emotions and remain calm under pres- sure is noticed by her team leader, who commends her improved leadership skills during stressful project phases.

Continued Growth:

Motivated by the positive changes, Maya explores deeperaspects of mindfulness. She joins a local meditation group to connect with others on similar paths and to deepen her prac- tice through community support. Maya also starts attending workshops on emotional intelligence to complement her mindfulness practice, enhancing her ability to understand and regulate her emotions effectively.

Reflection:

In her journal, Maya reflects on her journey, noting how mindfulness not only helped her manage stress but also enriched her personal and professional life. She feels more in control, centered, and mentally clear, which she attributes to her regular meditation and mindfulness exercises.

Maya's story illustrates the profound impact that mindfulnessand meditation can have on emotional regulation, particu- larly for young adults in high-pressure environments. By committing to regular practice and integrating mindfulness into daily life, Maya successfully transforms her approach to stress and emotional challenges, leading to enhanced well- being and professional growth.

Conclusion

Developing mindfulness and meditation is like giving your- self a superpower. It allows you to live more fully in the present moment, appreciate life more, and handle challenges with grace. By focusing on the here and now, you enhance your self-awareness, learning more about yourself and how you relate to the world around you. So, take a deep breath, focus on the present, and start your journey to a more mindful you. Remember, the journey of mindfulness is a path, not a destination, and every step, every breath, is a part of the adventure.

NOTES

SWEAT AND SMILES!

Embracing physical activity is like unlocking a secrettool that can help us navigate the rollercoaster of our emotions more smoothly. Just like a balanced diet feeds ourbody, regular exercise nourishes our emotional well-being. Here's a closer look at why getting moving is not just goodfor the body but also for the soul.

THE SCIENCE OF SWEAT AND SMILES

When we engage in physical activity, our body undergoes a series of remarkable changes, not just externally but internally too. Our heart pumps faster, our muscles work harder, and amidst this physical hustle, something magical happens in our brain. Chemicals known as endorphins, often calledthe body's "feel-good" hormones, are released. These are nature's mood lifters, providing us with a natural high, often referred to as the "runner's high." It's like the brain's way of giving us a high-five for taking care of our body.

STRESS BUSTERS IN ACTION

Exercise acts as a direct combatant against stress. Imagine each step during a run, each lift at the gym, or each stroke in the pool as physically pushing stress out of your body. Physical activity reduces levels of the body's stress hormones,such as adrenaline and cortisol. It's akin to turning down the volume on a loud, blaring alarm. With lower stress levels, the world seems a little brighter, a bit more manageable, enabling us to approach situations with a calmer, clearer mindset.

THE SLEEP CONNECTION

A hidden benefit of physical activity is its ability to improve our sleep quality. Like a natural sleep potion, regular exercisehelps us fall asleep faster and enjoy deeper sleep. Since sleep plays a critical role in emotional regulation, improving sleep quality is like giving our emotional resilience a nightly recharge, preparing us to face the next day's emotional challenges with renewed strength and clarity.

CONFIDENCE BOOSTER

Achieving physical goals can significantly boost our self-esteem. Every mile run, every pound lifted, and every game won is a testament to our capability and strength. This newfound confidence doesn't stay confined to the gym or the track; it spills over into other areas of our life. When we feel good about what our body can achieve, we start to viewemotional challenges through a lens of strength and resilience. It's as if by conquering physical challenges, we armourselves with the confidence to tackle emotional ones too.

A CONSTRUCTIVE OUTLET FOR FRUSTRATION

Physical activity offers a constructive way to release pent-up emotions like anger or frustration. Channeling these emotionsinto a workout is like turning negative energy into positive action. The transformation is twofold: we're not only diffusing these potent emotions but also benefiting our physical health in the process. It's a win-win situation.

SHARPENING THE MIND

Regular exercise doesn't just shape our body; it sharpens our mind. Improved concentration, sharper memory, and enhanced creativity are just some of the cognitive benefits linked to physical activity. This mental edge can be incrediblybeneficial for emotional regulation. With a sharper mind, we're better equipped to process our emotions, recognize what we're feeling, and why, and make informed, balanced decisions on how to react.

THE POWER OF CONNECTION

Many forms of physical activity also offer opportunities for social interaction, whether it's a team sport, a group fitness class, or just a walk with a friend. These social connectionscan provide emotional support and a sense of belonging. Knowing we're part of a community, that we're not tackling our fitness goals or emotional struggles alone, can provide a significant emotional lift.

ESTABLISHING A ROUTINE

Incorporating regular physical activity into our lives helps establish a routine, a rhythm to our day that can becomforting and stabilizing. This predictability helps reduce uncertainty and anxiety, making it easier to manage dailystresses and emotional fluctuations. A routine can be like an anchor, keeping us grounded amidst the stormy seas of emotion.

PHYSICAL ACTIVITY AS A JOURNEY

Embracing physical activity is more than just a series of exercises; it's a journey towards emotional balance and resilience. This journey is unique for everyone. For some, it might be about discovering a love for running; for others, it could be finding peace in yoga or excitement in dance. The key is to find an activity that you enjoy, something that makes you feelgood both physically and emotionally.

Conclusion

In a world that often feels like it's moving at lightning speed, where stress and anxiety have become common companions, embracing physical activity offers a beacon of hope. It's a testament to the power of movement, a reminder that bytaking care of our body, we're also taking care of our mind.

As we navigate through the highs and lows of life, incorporating physical activity into our routine can be a game- changer for emotional regulation. It's like equipping ourselves with a toolkit, ready to tackle whatever emotional challenges come our way. So, the next time you're feeling overwhelmed, consider taking a brisk walk, hitting the gym, or dancing to your favorite song. Your body (and your emotions) will thank you.

Scenario: Jamie learns to sweat and smile!

Jamie, a 22-year-old recent college graduate, is living in a small apartment in a bustling city, working an entry-level corporate job.

Jamie has always been known for her quick temper and impulsive reactions. Throughout college, these traits resulted in strained relationships and academic stress. After graduat- ing, Jamie recognized the need to develop better emotional regulation skills to succeed professionally and maintain personal relationships.

Act 1: Realization and Decision

- Jamie has an outburst at work after receiving constructive criticism from her supervisor. This incident nearly costs Jamie her job and serves as a wake-up call.
- Resolution: Jamie reflects on the incident and realizes the

need for change. She decides to tackle her emotional challenges by incorporating physical activity into her daily routine, as she remembers feeling calmer and more collected when she used to run in college.

Act 2: Implementation and Challenge

- Beginning: Jamie starts by jogging every morning. She struggles with consistency and motivation but persists, remembering the stakes involved.
- Middle: After a few weeks, Jamie starts to notice subtle changes. She feels less reactive at work and more contemplative. The physical exertion from jogging seems to be a physical outlet for her stress and frustration.
- Conflict: Despite initial improvements, a particularly stressful week at work triggers another emotional reaction from Jamie. She skips jogging for a few days, slipping back into old habits of snapping at colleagues.

Act 3: Adaptation and Growth

- Climax: Jamie feels tempted to give up after the setback but decides to address her emotional regulation more strategically. She diversifies her exercise routine by adding yoga twice a week to focus on mindfulness and breath control.

- Falling Action: This new combination strengthens Jamie's resilience. Yoga teaches her mindfulness which, when combined with jogging, significantly boosts her emotional control.
- Resolution: Jamie manages to handle a critical project at work with calm and leadership, receiving praise from her supervisor and peers. She reflects on her journey, realizing that the blend of physical exertion and mental discipline has been key to developing better emotional regulation.

Epilogue

- Reflection: Six months after starting her routine, Jamie has not only improved at work but has also mended and formed stronger personal relationships. She continues to explore other physical activities to keep her routine engaging and effective.
- Lesson: Jamie learns that emotional regulation can be significantly enhanced by physical discipline, which not only improves physical health but also mental and emotional stability.

This scenario outlines how a young adult can leverage an exercise routine to develop emotional regulation, illustrating the realistic challenges and triumphs involved in such a personal development journey.

HARNESSING URBAN RESOURCES FOR PHYSICAL ACTIVITY: A GUIDE FOR YOUNG ADULTS

In the vibrant landscape of city life, maintaining an active life-style can sometimes seem challenging due to the fast-paced environment and dense living conditions. However, towns and cities typically offer abundant resources that can help young adults engage in physical activities. This essay explores various avenues available to young adults seeking to incorporate more physical activity into their routines in an urban setting.

1. Utilizing Public Parks and Recreation Centers

Most cities boast a range of public parks which provide a free and accessible option for running, walking, and cycling. Larger parks often have designated fitness areas equipped with outdoor exercise machines or obstacle courses that can enhance one's workout regimen. Additionally, recreation centers offer facilities like swimming pools, basketball courts, and sports fields which are usually available for public use at little or no cost. These centers may also host fitness classes such as yoga, Pilates, or aerobics at discounted rates for local residents.

2. Joining Local Sports Leagues and Clubs

Participating in a sports league is a fantastic way to stay active and meet new people. Many cities host community sports leagues for soccer, basketball, ultimate frisbee, softball, and more. These leagues cater to all skill levels, from beginners to seasoned athletes. Additionally, specialized sports clubs like running groups, cycling clubs, or rowing clubs can provide structured opportunities for both improving fitness and socializing.

3. Enrolling in Fitness Classes and Gyms

Fitness classes are a popular way to stay fit and maintain motivation. Most urban areas have a diverse array of gyms and studios that offer classes ranging from spin and high- intensity interval training (HIIT) to more niche options like barre or kickboxing. Many gyms offer trial periods or free classes for first-timers, making it easier to explore different formats and find one that fits best.

4. Exploring Alternative Fitness Forms

For those looking for something different from traditional gym workouts, cities offer unique fitness experiences such as dance classes, martial arts studios, rock climbing gyms, and parkour facilities. These alternatives can make exercise feel more like a fun hobby rather than a chore, greatly enhancing the appeal of regular physical activity.

5. Biking and Walking as Transportation

Incorporating physical activity into daily routines can be as simple as choosing to walk or bike rather than driving or using public transportation. Many urban areas are enhancing their infrastructure to be more pedestrian and cyclist-friendly,offering bike lanes and improved sidewalks. Utilizing these facilities not only contributes to physical health but also reduces one's carbon footprint.

6. Taking Advantage of Water Sports

For cities near bodies of water—like lakes, rivers, or oceans— water sports can be an excellent way to exercise. Kayaking, paddleboarding, sailing, and swimming are great for full- body workouts and can be a refreshing alternative to land- based activities. Local marinas or boating clubs often provide rentals and lessons, making these sports accessible to beginners.

7. Engaging with Technology-Aided Fitness

Technology offers new ways to engage in physical activity through virtual fitness classes and mobile apps that guide outdoor exercises like running or interval training. Apps can also track progress, set goals, and provide customized workout plans. This is especially useful for those who prefer aself-guided approach but need a bit of structure and motivation.

Conclusion

Cities are filled with opportunities for young adults to stay active, offering a wide range of options from traditional sports and fitness classes to innovative and unconventional physical activities. By leveraging these urban resources, individuals can easily integrate physical activity into their daily lives, enhancing both their physical and mental health. Exploring these options can not only help in maintaining an active lifestyle but also connect individuals with their community and the unique offerings of their urban environment. By taking the initiative and exploring these diverse resources, young adults can enjoy a healthier, more active life amidst the hustle and bustle of city living.

NOTES

SETTING AND ACCOMPLISHING GOALS

Setting and accomplishing goals is like embarking on a treasure hunt. The map is your plan, the treasure represents your ambitions, and the journey is the path to achieving your dreams. For young adults, learning to navigate this journey effectively is crucial for self-regulation and overall development. It's about learning to steer your own ship, make your own choices, and take responsibility for your future. Let's explore the habits you can develop to set and accomplish your goals, turning your visions into reality.

UNDERSTANDING GOAL SETTING

Goal setting involves identifying something you want to achieve and then laying out a step-by-step plan to reach it. It's like setting a destination in your GPS before starting to drive. Without a destination, you might end up going in circles, but with one, you can take the most efficient route and track your progress along the way.

WHY SET GOALS?

- **Provides Direction:** Goals give you a sense of direction, making it easier to focus on what's important.
- **Boosts Motivation:** Setting and achieving goals provides a sense of accomplishment that boosts your motivation to tackle

new challenges.

- **Improves Self-Confidence:** Every goal achieved builds confidence in your abilities, encouraging youto set and achieve even more ambitious goals.

- **Enhances Self-Discipline:** The process of workingtowards a goal helps develop self-discipline, an essential skill for self-regulation and success in life.

Let's dive into a hypothetical scenario that showcases how a young adult, Mia, enhances her emotional regulation by setting clear goals.

Scenario: Mia's Journey to Goal-Setting and Emotional Regulation

Before: Mia, a high school junior, often found herself over-whelmed by stress and anxiety due to her busy schedule. Balancing schoolwork, soccer practice, and her part-time job felt like juggling too many balls at once. She noticed that her stress levels would skyrocket, especially before exams or soccer matches, leading to sleepless nights and irritability.Mia realized she needed a change but wasn't sure where to start.

The Turning Point: One evening, after a particularly stressfulday, Mia confided in her older brother, Alex, who had gone through similar challenges. Alex shared how setting specific goals helped him manage his time and emotions better. Inspired by their conversation, Mia decided to give it a try.

Setting Goals: Mia started by setting aside some quiet time to think about what she wanted to achieve in the next few months. She identified three main areas to focus on: improving her grades, performing well in soccer, and finding more time to relax and unwind. For each area, she set specific,measurable goals:

- **Academic:** To improve her grades, Mia aimed to dedicate two hours each night to homework and study, focusing especially on math, her weakest subject.
- **Soccer:** To enhance her soccer skills, she committed to practicing penalty kicks for an extra 30 minutes after team practice twice a week.
- **Personal Well-being:** To ensure she had time to relax, Mia decided to spend at least one hour on the weekend doing something she enjoyed, like reading or going for a bike ride.

Action Plan: With her goals set, Mia created a weekly schedule that balanced her schoolwork, soccer practice, job, and personal time. She used a planner to organize her tasks and track her progress.

Emotional Regulation: As Mia began working toward her goals, she noticed a significant shift in her stress levels. By breaking down her big challenges into smaller, manageable goals, she felt more in control of her life. This sense of control reduced her anxiety, and she found it easier to keep her emotions in check, even when faced with setbacks. Mia also started using breathing exercises as a quick way to calm down whenever she felt overwhelmed.

Reflection and Adjustment: Every two weeks, Mia reviewed her progress and adjusted her goals and strategies as needed. This reflection helped her stay flexible and responsive to her own needs, further enhancing her emotional regulation.

Outcome: Over time, Mia's grades improved, she scored more goals in soccer, and, most importantly, she felt happier and less stressed. She learned that by setting clear, achievable goals, she could not only improve her performance but also manage her emotions more effectively.

Conclusion: Mia's story illustrates the power of goal-setting in enhancing emotional regulation. By identifying her priori- ties, setting specific targets, and creating a plan of action, she was able to reduce stress and navigate her challenges with greater ease and confidence. Mia's experience shows that with the right goals and a bit of planning, young adults can take control of their emotions and achieve success in various aspects of their lives.

HABITS TO DEVELOP FOR SETTING AND ACCOMPLISHING GOALS

1. Be Specific and Realistic

A clear, specific goal is easier to achieve than a vague one. "Improve my grades" is less actionable than "Achieve a B or better in math." Ensure your goals are realistic; setting unattainable goals can lead to disappointment and discourage you from setting new ones.

Action Step: For each goal, define what success looks like and ensure it's something within your control and capabilities.

2. Break Goals into Smaller Steps

Large goals can feel overwhelming. Breaking them down into smaller, manageable tasks makes them less daunting and easier to tackle.

Action Step: List the steps needed to achieve each goal and focus on completing one step at a time.

3. Set Deadlines

Deadlines create a sense of urgency, helping you stay focused and motivated. They also help you track your progress.

Action Step: Assign a realistic deadline to each goal and its steps. Use a calendar or planner to keep track.

74

4. Write Down Your Goals

Writing down your goals makes them real and tangible. It's a physical reminder of what you're working towards.

Action Step: Keep a goal journal or use a digital app to record your goals, progress, and reflections.

5. Visualize Success

Visualization is a powerful tool. Imagining yourself achieving your goals can boost your motivation and confidence.

Action Step: Spend a few minutes each day visualizing your success. Imagine how it feels to achieve your goals.

6. Embrace Failure as a Learning Opportunity

Failure is a part of the process. Each setback teaches you something new and brings you one step closer to your goal.

Action Step: When you encounter failure, reflect on what went wrong and how you can improve. Then, adjust your plan and keep moving forward.

7. Seek Support and Accountability

Sharing your goals with friends, family, or mentors can provide you with support and motivation. They can also hold you accountable, helping you stay on track.

Action Step: Choose an accountability partner and share your goals and progress with them.

8. Celebrate Milestones

Recognizing and celebrating each step you complete towards your goal can boost your motivation and enjoyment of the journey.

Action Step: Reward yourself for reaching milestones. The rewards should be meaningful and reinforce your progress.

9. Stay Flexible

Sometimes, circumstances change, and your goals may need to be adjusted. Being flexible allows you to adapt and remain committed to your overall vision.

Action Step: Regularly review your goals and make adjustments as needed to reflect your current situation andpriorities.

10. Cultivate Positive Habits and Routines

Consistent habits and routines provide a structure that can help you work towards your goals every day without having to rely solely on motivation.

Action Step: Develop daily or weekly habits that move you closer to your goals, and incorporate them into your routine.

Sample Reflection Questions:

- What worked well? _____
- What challenges did I face? _____
- How did I overcome them? _____

Conclusion

Setting and achieving goals is a dynamic process that requires clarity, commitment, and adaptability. By developing these habits, young adults can enhance their ability to self-regulate, laying a strong foundation for personal and professional success. Remember, the journey towards your goals is just as important as the destination. Each step teaches you about yourself, what you're capable of, and how you can continually grow and improve. Start small, stay focused, and celebrate your progress. Your dreams are within reach, one goal at a time. Need a clear worksheet to help stay organized?

Turn the page!

GOAL OVERVIEW

Goal: [Write a clear and concise statement of your goal.]

Importance: [Why is this goal important to you? What impact will it have on your life or career?]

SMART Goals Criteria

Specific	Measurable	Achievable	Relevant	Time-bound
[What exactly do you want to achieve?]	[How will you measure success?]	[Is the goal realistic?]	[Does this goal align with your broader life or career goals?]	[What is your deadline for achieving this goal?]

Action Plan

Step 1: [First action step]

- **Deadline**: [Date]
- **Resources Needed**: [What do you need to complete this step?]

Step 2: [Second action step]

- **Deadline**: [Date]
- **Resources Needed**: [What do you need to complete this step?]

Step 3: [Continue as needed]

- **Deadline**: [Date]
- **Resources Needed**: [What do you need to complete this step?]

Progress Review

Date: [Schedule regular review dates]

- **Achievements**: [What have you accomplished by thisdate?]

- **Adjustments**: [What changes are necessary moving forward?]

NOTES

CREATIVE OUTLETS

Engaging in creative activities is like having a secret doorway to a playground where your emotions can run free, explore, and express themselves in safe and constructive ways. These activities, whether it's drawing, writing, playing music, or crafting, offer a unique avenue for managing and understanding your feelings. Here's why diving into creativity is so beneficial for emotional regulation:

Provides an Outlet for Expression: Sometimes, our emotions are too complex or overwhelming to put into words. Creative activities offer an alternative language for expression. It's like having a conversation without needing to speak; you can pour your feelings into your artwork, music, or writing, which can be incredibly relieving and therapeutic.

Reduces Stress: Getting lost in a creative project is like taking a mini-vacation from your worries. The focus required can help clear your mind of stress and anxiety, similar to the calm feeling you get when watching waves at the beach or stars in the night sky. This break from stress is crucial for emotional regulation, allowing you to return to your emotions with a refreshed perspective.

•• **Boosts Self-Esteem:** Creating something from your own imagination is empowering. It's like leveling upin a video game;

each achievement boosts your confidence. This increased self-esteem can help you approach emotional challenges with a stronger senseof self and resilience.

- **Encourages Mindfulness:** Engaging in creative activities requires you to be fully present in the moment, much like mindfulness practices. When you're focused on painting a scene or writing a story,you're anchored in the now, paying attention to details and sensations. This mindfulness can decreasefeelings of anxiety and depression, contributing to better emotional regulation.

- **Facilitates Problem-Solving:** Creativity is all about thinking outside the box and exploring new solutions. This mindset doesn't just apply to your projects but also to personal challenges, including emotional ones. By practicing creative thinking, you can become better at finding unique ways to cope with and regulate your emotions.

- **Builds Connections:** Sharing your creative work can lead to positive social interactions, whether it's through compliments, constructive feedback, or just the act of sharing something personal. These connections reinforce a sense of belonging and support, which are essential for emotional well-being.
- **Encourages Positive Emotions:** Lastly, the joy and satisfaction

of creating something can spark positive emotions like happiness, pride, and a sense of accomplishment. These positive feelings can counterbalance negative emotions, helping to regulate your overall mood.

In essence, engaging in creative activities is like having a toolkit for emotional regulation. It offers a constructive way to express and understand your feelings, reduces stress, boosts self-esteem, and even connects you with others. So, whether you're painting, writing, making music, or crafting, you're not just creating art; you're crafting a more emotion- ally balanced self.

Scenario: Eddie's Creative Journey: Exploring Self-Discovery Through Art

In today's fast-paced world filled with new technologies and endless work, people often forget to focus on understanding themselves. Eddie, a 24-year-old software developer, was one of these people. His life was organized and predictable, full of coding and fixing bugs in his programs. But deep down, he felt something was missing.

A Change Begins

Eddie's daily life was highly structured, from his work schedule to his coffee breaks. Yet, despite his success, he felt an emptiness inside. This feeling of being lost changed one morning during his usual commute to work while listening to a podcast called "Creative

Living Beyond Fear." The podcast talked about using creativity to improve oneself, and it strucka chord with Eddie. He realized that he could find out more about himself by trying new, creative things.

• Stepping Into Creativity

Eddie decided to try something completely different from his work: pottery. This was a big change from the precise and orderly world of computer code. Working with clay was messy and the results were often imperfect, but Eddie learned to appreciate the beauty of the process itself, not just the finished product.

He didn't stop there. Eddie began to write. At first, he wrote blogs related to technology, but soon he was writing poems and short stories. Writing helped him reflect on his own thoughts and feelings, and each word helped him understand himself better.

• Combining Two Worlds

As Eddie spent more time being creative, he noticed that he felt happier and more relaxed. The quiet time spent molding clay and writing poems helped clear his mind and made him better at handling stress. These benefits weren't just personal; they improved his work performance too. Eddie started to use creative ideas to solve technical problems at work. He even created a new software that got him a lot of praise from his coworkers.

- ## **Growth and Understanding**

What started as a small experiment in creativity became a key part of Eddie's life. It helped him learn more about himself and find a balance between his work and personal life. Eddie's journey shows us that being creative can help anyone understand themselves better and make their lives more fulfilling.

- ## **Conclusion**

Eddie's story is a powerful example of how stepping out of your comfort zone and trying new things can lead to personal growth. It reminds us that in our busy lives, it's important to take time for creative activities. They are not just hobbies, but essential parts of discovering who we are and living a balanced life. As Eddie continues to explore his new interests, they provide him not only with joy but also with a fresh perspective on life. His growth from a programmer to a more creative and fulfilled individual highlights the powerful impact of art and creativity in finding oneself.

EXPLORING CREATIVE OUTLETS FOR YOUNG ADULTS IN URBAN SETTINGS

In the bustling dynamics of urban environments, young adults often seek creative outlets to express themselves, learn new skills, and connect with like-minded individuals. Urban centers, with their rich cultural tapestries and diverse popula- tions, offer a myriad of opportunities for creative exploration. This essay delves into various strategies and resources that can facilitate the pursuit of creative activities in towns and cities.

1.Local Libraries: Gateways to Creativity

Local libraries are treasure troves of free resources. They offer not only books but also magazines, DVDs, and access to online courses related to different arts and crafts. Many libraries host free workshops, writer's clubs, and art classes. They sometimes provide access to digital creation tools, including software for video editing, graphic design, and even music production. Thus, libraries serve as an essential first step for young adults looking to explore creative avenues without financial burden.

2.Community Centers and Cultural Hubs

Community centers and cultural hubs often offer classes and workshops in disciplines ranging from pottery and painting to dance and drama. These institutions provide not just the space to learn, but also the chance to engage with community members who share similar interests. They are invaluable in promoting cultural activities that might be underrepresented in mainstream outlets, providing a platform for cultural expression and community building.

3.Educational Institutions

Local colleges and universities can be excellent resources for creative pursuits. Many institutions allow non-students to attend courses for a nominal fee. They also host guest lectures, art exhibitions, and film screenings that can provide inspiration and education to young adults. Additionally, these settings offer networking opportunities with profes- sionals and educators who can provide guidance, mentor- ship, and the potential for collaborative projects.

4.Online Platforms

In the digital age, the internet is a pivotal resource for finding creative outlets. Websites like Meetup.com enable individuals to find local groups or events based on specific interests such as photography, writing, or knitting. Social media platforms like Instagram and Pinterest can also offer inspiration and connect young adults with global art communities. Furthermore, platforms such as YouTube provide extensive tutorials that can help in honing one's skills at home.

5.Art Cooperatives and Shared Spaces

Joining an art cooperative or utilizing a shared space can provide access to expensive resources like kilns for pottery, looms for weaving, or studios for recording music. These spaces often operate on membership models, making them more affordable. Shared creative spaces not only facilitate artistic endeavors but also foster a sense of community and collaboration, which can be hugely beneficial for personal and professional growth.

6.Volunteering for Art Organizations

Volunteering for arts festivals, local theater productions, or community art projects can provide practical experience, which is invaluable. Such involvement also enhances one's resume and can open doors to future employment opportuni- ties in creative fields. Volunteering allows for a deeper connection with the cultural ecosystem and can be a rich source of inspiration and learning.

7.Public Spaces and Street Art

Many cities embrace public art and offer legal graffiti walls, outdoor pianos, and art installations. Engaging with these spaces can stimulate creativity and offer unique modes of expression. Public spaces are especially important for art forms like performance art or flash mobs, which rely on spon-taneous and public participation.

Conclusion

For young adults living in towns or cities, the opportunities for engaging in creative activities are as vast as one's imagina- tion. From traditional resources like libraries and educational institutions to modern platforms such as digital media and shared creative spaces, the urban environment is ripe with potential for artistic exploration. By leveraging these resources, young adults can enrich their creative lives, foster community connections, and contribute to the vibrant cultural fabric of their urban centers. Engaging actively in these opportunities not only enhances personal growth but also strengthens the community by promoting diverse cultural expressions.

NOTES

SEEKING FEEDBACK

The next step to enhancing self-awareness is like unlocking a secret level in a video game where you

gain special insights that help you understand yourself from the outside in. This secret level is called "seeking feedback." Feedback is like a mirror that reflects how others see us, our actions, and our behaviors. It's important because sometimes we're too close to ourselves to see the whole picture. Just like artists sometimes step back from their paintings to see their work from a new perspective, we need feedback to step back and view ourselves more clearly.

WHAT IS FEEDBACK?

Feedback is information given to you by others about how your actions and behaviors are perceived. It can come from friends, family, teachers, coaches, or anyone you interact with regularly. Feedback can be positive, telling you what you're doing well, or constructive, suggesting areas where you can improve.

WHY IS SEEKING FEEDBACK IMPORTANT?

- **Growth and Improvement:** Feedback points out areas we might not realize need improvement. It's like a coach giving you tips to improve your game. You might not notice a mistake you're making until someone points it out.

- **Understanding** How Others See Us: Sometimes, there's a difference between how we see ourselves and how others see us. Feedback helps bridge that gap, making us more aware of our impact on others. Building Stronger Relationships: When you ask for feedback, it shows that you value others' opinions and are open to growth. This openness can strengthen your relationships.

- **Boosting** Confidence: Positive feedback can boost your confidence by highlighting your strengths. Even constructive feedback can be empowering, as it gives you a clear path to become even better.

HOW TO SEEK FEEDBACK

1.Ask Directly

The simplest way to get feedback is to ask for it directly. You could ask your teacher how you can improve your essays, or ask a friend how you've been as a friend. Be specific in your questions to get useful answers.

2.Create a Safe Space

People might be hesitant to give honest feedback if they're worried about hurting your feelings. Let them know you appreciate their honesty and that you're seeking feedback to learn and grow.

3.Listen Openly

When receiving feedback, listen without interrupting or getting defensive. Remember, the goal is to learn about your- self, even if some of what you hear might be tough to accept.

4.Reflect on the Feedback

After receiving feedback, take some time to think about it. Ask yourself if it aligns with your self-perception and what you can learn from it.

5.Act on the Feedback

Feedback is most valuable when you use it to make changes. If multiple people suggest the same area for improvement, that's a strong signal it's something you should work on.

Here's a Scenario: Tyler's anger

Imagine Tyler, a high school junior who's known among his friends for being quick to anger. He doesn't really get why, until one day, his best friend, Alex, points out that Tyler tends to snap whenever he feels embarrassed or put on the spot, especially in group settings. Tyler hadn't noticed this pattern, but hearing it from Alex sparked a bit of self-awareness.

Strategy: Tyler decides to seek more feedback, not just from Alex but from others close to him, about how he reacts in different situations. He asks specific questions like, "Can you tell me about a time when I reacted angrily, and what do you think triggered it?"

Through these conversations, Tyler learns that his anger often masks feelings of insecurity or fear of looking foolish.

After: Armed with this feedback, Tyler starts paying closer attention to his emotional state, especially in social situations. He begins to recognize the early signs of embarrassment or insecurity and uses techniques like taking deep breaths and reminding himself that making mistakes is okay and doesn't reflect on his worth. Over time, Tyler's friends notice he's become more relaxed and less prone to outbursts. They feel more comfortable around him, leading to deeper and more open friendships.

Tyler's story shows how seeking feedback can shine a light on our blind spots, helping us understand our emotional triggers better. This awareness is the first step toward managing our reactions and improving our emotional regulation.

HANDLING FEEDBACK

Receiving feedback, especially if it's not all positive, can be challenging. Here's how to handle it:

- **Stay Calm:** Keep your emotions in check. It's okay to feel upset but try not to react impulsively.

- **Don't Take It Personally:** Try to see feedback as about your behavior, not your character. It's not aboutwho you are as a person, but about how you can grow.

Thank for the Feedback: Always thank the personfor their feedback, even if you don't agree with it. Acknowledging their effort to help you shows maturity and respect.

- **Seek Clarification:** If the feedback isn't clear, ask for examples or more details. This can help you understand the feedback better and how to apply it.

TIPS FOR EFFECTIVE FEEDBACK SEEKING

- **Specific:** Instead of asking, "How did I do?" ask, "What's one thing I could have done better in my presentation?"

- **Choose the Right People:** Seek feedback from people who know you well and whose opinions you respect. **Use Feedback as a Tool, Not a Weapon:** Feedback is a tool for self-improvement, not a weapon to be used against you or others. Approach it with a positive mindset.

Conclusion

Seeking feedback is a brave step towards enhancing self-awareness and emotional regulation. It's like putting together a puzzle — each piece of feedback adds to the picture of who you are and how you can grow. Remember, the goal of seeking feedback isn't to become perfect but to become better, one step at a time. By being open to feedback, you're showing courage, humility, and a commitment to personal growth. So, take a deep breath, ask for that feedback, and embark on the exciting journey of discovering and improving yourself.

NOTES

94

ACTIVE LISTENING SKILLS

Practicing active listening is like tuning your radio comes to your favorite station, where the music or the news through clearly, without any static or interference. It's about fully concentrating on what is being said rather than just passively hearing the message of the speaker. Active listening involves listening with all senses and engaging with the speaker both verbally and non-verbally. Here's why it's so important and how you can get better at it:

WHY PRACTICE ACTIVE LISTENING?

Active listening can be a powerful tool for emotional regulation, much like having a trusty map helps you navigate through unfamiliar territory without getting lost. When youactively listen, you're not just hearing words; you're fully engaging with someone's thoughts and feelings, and this process can have a profound effect on managing your own emotions. Here's how:

- **Increases Empathy:** Active listening helps you put yourself in someone else's shoes, seeing the world from their perspective. This is like watching a movie from the viewpoint of the main character; you feel what they feel and understand their challenges and triumphs. This empathy can cool down your emotional responses, helping you react more calmly and thoughtfully in emotional situations.

- **Lowers Stress:** Have you ever noticed that when you focus intently on something like a captivating book or a challenging puzzle, your worries seem to fade away? Active listening has a similar effect. By concentrating on understanding another person, your mind takes a break from your stressors. This break can help regulate your emotions, reducing feelings of anxiety or being overwhelmed.

- **Improves Problem-Solving:** Active listening often involves hearing about problems or challenges from others. As you process this information and think about constructive responses or advice, you're also learning to approach your problems with a more balanced perspective. It's like practicing a sport; the more you do it, the better you get. In this case, you're practicing emotional balance and resilience.

- **Encourages Open Communication**: When you listen actively, you're not just being a good listener; you're also creating an environment where open, honest communication is valued. This openness can make it easier for you to express your own emotions in a healthy way, reducing the likelihood of pent-up feelings that can lead to emotional outbursts. It's akin to opening windows in a stuffy room, letting fresh air in and making the environment more pleasant.

Builds Stronger Relationships: Strong relationships are a key factor in emotional well-being. Active listening strengthens bonds with others, making you feel supported and understood. This sense of connection can be a powerful source of emotional stability. Imagine having a safety net; knowing it's there can make you feel more secure as you walk the tightrope of life.

In summary, active listening helps with emotional regulation by increasing empathy, lowering stress, improving problem- solving skills, encouraging open communication, and building stronger relationships. It's like having a toolkit for navigating the emotional landscape of life more effectively, helping you maintain your balance no matter what terrain you encounter.

STEPS TO BUILD ACTIVE LISTENING:

How to Practice Active Listening:

- **Give Full Attention to the Speaker:** Imagine you're a photographer focusing your camera on a subject.

Everything else becomes blurry. When you listen actively, focus all your attention on the speaker. Put away distractions like your phone or thoughts about what you're going to say next.

- **Show That You're Listening:** Non-verbal cues like nodding your head, making eye contact, and leaning slightly forward show the speaker you're engaged. It's like clapping at the end of a performance; it shows appreciation for the effort.

- **Provide Feedback:** Reflection is a part of active listening. It's like echoing back what someone said in your own words, like giving someone a summary of a story they just told you to make sure you got it right. This can include asking questions to clarify certain points or simply paraphrasing what was said to demonstrate understanding.

- **Defer Judgment:** Keeping an open mind is crucial. It's like reading a book without skipping to the last page. Wait until the speaker is finished before forming an opinion or offering advice. This ensures you have all the information and understand the context before responding.

- **Respond Appropriately:** Active listening is completed by an appropriate response. It's acknowledging the speaker's feelings and respectfully offering your thoughts. Think of it as adding your brushstroke to a collaborative painting. Your response should contribute positively to the conversation.

By practicing active listening, you're not just hearing words; you're engaging in a meaningful exchange of ideas. It increases emotional regulation and self-awareness by making you more in tune with the feelings and perspectives of others as well as your responses to them. Just like learning any new skill, it takes practice. But over time, active listening can become second nature, enriching your interactions andunderstanding of the world around you.

Scenario: Alex's Path to Emotional Regulation Through Active Listening

Background:

Alex, a 25-year-old customer support representative, often finds himself in the middle of stressful customer interactions. While he tries to solve problems efficiently, his quick temper and tendency to interrupt have led to misunderstandings and unresolved issues. After receiving constructive feedback from his supervisor about his communication style, Alex decides to improve his emotional regulation by practicing active listening.

The Incident That Sparked Change:

During a particularly busy day, Alex found himself handling a complicated complaint from a frustrated customer. In his usual manner, Alex began formulating his response while the customer was still explaining the problem, leading to a heated exchange where the customer felt unheard and Alex felt attacked. This interaction ended with the customer requesting to speak with a manager, leaving Alex embar-rassed and determined to make a change.

Adopting Active Listening:

Alex starts his journey by researching active listening techniques. He learns about the importance of fully concentrating, understanding, responding, and then remembering what is being said, instead of passively hearing the speaker's words. Alex commits to practicing these skills both in and out of work to better manage his emotional responses.

Practice Makes Perfect:

Alex begins by reminding himself before each call to clear his mind and focus solely on the customer's words. He makes a conscious effort to not plan his responses while listening. Instead, he nods in agreement, makes occasional notes, and uses phrases like "I see," "Please go on," or "Can you explain abit more?" to encourage the customer and show that he is attentive.

Challenges and Learning:

One of Alex's biggest challenges is controlling his impulse to interrupt when he thinks he already knows the solution. During a call with a particularly long-winded customer, he catches himself losing patience. However, he manages to hold back, allowing the customer to fully express their concerns, which surprisingly leads to Alex discovering a misunder- standing in the customer's account settings—a detail he might have missed had he interrupted.

Applying Skills in High-Pressure Situations:

A month into his practice, Alex faces a true test of his skills during a major service outage, a situation ripe with angry calls. Using active listening, Alex is able to de-escalate situa- tions more effectively. By truly understanding the customers' issues and reflecting their feelings back to them, he helpsthem feel valued and understood, which diminishes their anger and allows for more productive conversations.

Positive Feedback:

As Alex's ability to listen actively improves, so does the quality of his interactions. Customers start to leave positive feedback about how understood and supported they feel, which boosts Alex's confidence and validates his efforts. His supervisor notices the change and commends Alex for his improved performance and professionalism.

Broader Impacts:

Encouraged by his success at work, Alex starts using active listening with his family and friends, leading to better personal relationships. He finds that he is able to stay calmer in potentially volatile situations because he better under- stands the perspectives of others.

Reflection:

In his reflection during a team meeting, Alex shares his journey and how active listening not only transformed his professional interactions but also helped him regulate his emotional responses more effectively. He feels more in controland capable of handling stressful situations without losing histemper.

Alex's commitment to practicing active listening reshapes his approach to communication, enabling him to manage his emotions better and improve his interactions. This journey highlights the power of active listening in enhancing emotional intelligence and fostering positive relationships, both personally and professionally.

NOTES

EXPLORING NEW EXPERIENCES

Exploring new experiences is like diving into a treasure hunt where each adventure adds a piece to the puzzle of who you are. This journey isn't just about the excitement or the stories you'll tell; it's also about how these experiences shape your ability to manage your emotions.

Here's why venturing into the unknown can be a boon for your emotional regulation:

- **Expands Your Comfort Zone**: Think of your comfort zone as a small circle around you. Everything inside is familiar and safe, but stepping outside introduces you to the unknown. Each new experience stretches this circle a bit wider, making what was once daunting feel manageable. This process is like training your emotional muscles to handle uncertainty and change more gracefully, reducing anxiety or fear over time.

- Builds Resilience: Facing new challenges and learning to navigate unfamiliar situations is like adding tools to your emotional toolbox. Sometimes you might stumble, but each time you get back up, you're building resilience. This resilience helps you bounce back from setbacks more quickly, making you less likely to be overwhelmed by negative emotions. Enhances Problem-Solving Skills: Every new experience is a problem to solve or a puzzle to piece together. Whether it's figuring out how to communicate in a foreign language or learning to cook a new dish, you're constantly thinking on your feet. This sharpens your problem-solving skills, which can be applied to emotional challenges, helping you find creative solutions to personal conflicts or stressful situations.

- Provides New Perspectives: Exploring new experiences can shift the way you see the world and yourself. It's like climbing a mountain and looking back at the path you've taken; the view from the top can give you a new appreciation for your journey and the obstacles you've overcome. This broader perspective can make your problems seem smaller and more manageable, aiding in emotional regulation.

- Increases Self-Awareness: As you navigate new experiences, you learn more about your likes, dislikes, strengths, and weaknesses. This self-awareness is key to understanding your emotional responses. It's like being the author of your own story; the more you understand your character, the better you can navigate the plot twists of life.

- **Promotes Joy and Fulfillment:** New experiences often bring joy, excitement, and a sense of accomplishment. These positive emotions can act as a counterbalance to stress, anxiety, and sadness, promoting a more balanced emotional state. Imagine adding vibrant colors to a painting; the more hues you have, the more nuanced and beautiful the artwork becomes.

Scenario: Zoe's story

Let's explore the story of Zoe, a 20-year-old who has recently started her career in a bustling city. Zoe, having always lived in a small, close-knit community, finds the transition to city life and her new job overwhelming. To cope with the stress and navigate her new environment, Zoe decides to challenge herself by joining a rock climbing gym, a decision that trans- forms her life in ways she never anticipated.

Expanding the Comfort Zone

At first, Zoe is hesitant. The idea of scaling walls and trusting her safety to ropes and harnesses is far removed from anything she's ever done. Her initial attempts are shaky, and the height makes her nervous. But with each session, Zoe becomes more comfortable with the discomfort, pushing her boundaries a little further each time. This new hobby forces her to confront her fears head-on, expanding her comfortzone not just in rock climbing but in her personal and profes- sional life as well.

Building Resilience

Zoe's journey up the climbing wall is not without its falls. Each slip and missed grip is a setback, but it's also a lesson. She learns to analyze what went wrong, to get back up, andto try again with a revised strategy. This resilience spills over into her work, where Zoe starts to approach challenges with renewed grit, viewing failures as stepping stones rather than roadblocks.

Enhancing Problem-Solving Skills

Rock climbing is as much a mental exercise as it is physical. Zoe learns to look at the wall and visualize her path, consid- ering which holds will support her weight and which moves are within her reach. This strategic planning and quick thinking help enhance her problem-solving skills, which prove invaluable in navigating the complexities of her newjob and city life.

Providing New Perspectives

From the top of the climbing wall, Zoe sees the world differ- ently—literally and metaphorically. The physical height offersa new viewpoint of her surroundings, while the accomplish- ment of reaching the top gives her a fresh perspective onwhat she's capable of achieving. It's a reminder that some- times you need to take a step back (or climb up) to see the bigger picture in life and work.

Increasing Self-Awareness

Through rock climbing, Zoe becomes more attuned to her body's signals and her mind's responses to stress and fear. This heightened self-awareness helps her recognize when she's pushing her limits too far and when she needs to take a break, both on the wall and in her career. Understanding her strengths and weaknesses better, Zoe learns to leverage them to her advantage.

Promoting Joy and Fulfillment

Despite the initial fear and the physical strain, rock climbing brings Zoe immense joy and a sense of fulfillment. Each climb is a personal victory, a tangible measure of her growth and perseverance. This new source of happiness becomes a vital counterbalance to the stresses of her professional life, teaching her the importance of finding and pursuing passions outside of work.

Zoe's story illustrates how stepping out of one's comfort zone and embracing new challenges can significantly impact emotional regulation and overall well-being. Through rock climbing, she expands her comfort zone, builds resilience, enhances problem-solving skills, gains new perspectives, increases self-awareness, and finds joy and fulfillment— demonstrating that exploring new experiences is a powerful tool for personal and professional development.

DISCOVERING NEW EXPERIENCES: A GUIDE FOR YOUNG ADULTS IN URBAN ENVIRONMENTS

Urban centers, with their eclectic mix of cultures, interests, and activities, provide fertile grounds for young adults eager to explore new experiences. The city offers a kaleidoscope of possibilities that can enrich life, expand horizons, and intro- duce individuals to diverse cultures and hobbies. This essay provides practical suggestions on how and where young adults can find resources to explore new experiences in their town or city.

1.Cultural Festivals and Local Events

Cities are vibrant with festivals that range from music and film to food and art. These events are perfect for experiencing different cultures and art forms. Young adults can check local event calendars, city official websites, and community bulletin boards to find details about upcoming festivals. Engaging in these events not only enriches one's cultural understanding but also provides opportunities to meet new people and learn new things.

2.Meetup Groups and Social Clubs

Platforms like Meetup.com offer a plethora of groups tailored to specific interests, hobbies, and activities. Whether it's a hiking club, a tech enthusiasts group, or a book discussion club, these gatherings are invaluable for exploring new avenues. Social clubs provide a structured way to engage with a hobby and connect with individuals who share similar interests, making the city's vastness more personal and accessible.

3.Volunteer Opportunities

Volunteering can open doors to experiences that are both rewarding and enriching. Many organizations in cities need volunteers for various roles, including cultural institutions like museums, community gardens, or local charities. This not only helps one give back to the community but also exposes one to new environments and skills. Websites like VolunteerMatch can connect individuals with organizations in need of help.

4.Recreational Sports Leagues

Many cities have recreational sports leagues that range from soccer and basketball to less conventional sports like ultimate frisbee or kickball. These leagues are a great way to stayactive, meet people, and engage in a bit of friendly competi- tion. Local sports and recreation departments often have information on how to join these leagues or where to watch the games.

5.Art Collectives and Creative Workshops

Urban areas are hubs for creative expression. Art collectives and local workshops offer classes that can range from painting and sculpture to digital art and DIY crafts. These workshops not only teach new skills but also connect partici- pants with the local art scene. Checking out local art supply stores or community centers can provide leads on these creative outlets.

6.Exploration Through Cuisine

Cities offer a vast array of culinary experiences from around the world. Exploring local markets, food trucks, and ethnic restaurants can expose one to global cultures and cuisines without ever leaving the city. Many communities also offer cooking classes for specific types of cuisine, which can be an enjoyable way to learn about the culture behind the food.

7.Local Libraries and Bookstores

Libraries and bookstores often host free lectures, author readings, and book clubs that can provide intellectual stimulation and a chance to engage with thoughtful communities. These venues also frequently serve as a hub for information on localevents and classes, making them a valuable resource for anyone looking to expand their horizons.

8.Exploring Nature

Even the most urban areas have pockets of nature, whether it's city parks, river walks, or botanical gardens. These spaces offer a respite from urban life and a chance to partake in outdoor activities such as bird-watching, nature walks, orsimply enjoying a picnic with friends.

For young adults in urban areas, the city is a canvas, ready to be explored. From cultural festivals and social clubs to volun-teer opportunities and sports leagues, the possibilities for discovering new experiences are limitless. By stepping out of one's comfort zone and engaging actively with the resources available, young adults can fully experience the richness of urban life, meet diverse groups of people, and develop new interests that enrich their lives profoundly. The key is to be open and proactive in seeking out these opportunities, which are plentiful in any bustling city.

NOTES

PART TWO

POSITIVE OUTCOMES OF DEVELOPING
THESE SKILLS

OUTCOME

O nce a young adult has developed stronger self-awareness by recognizing their emotions, understanding their triggers, reflecting or thinking back, exercising mindfulness & medita- tion, and seeking feedback, they will enjoy desired outcomes of emotional regulation that can truly be life-changing.

We will discuss SIX desirable outcomes here:

Enhanced Relationships Academic & Professional SuccessBetter Decision Making Increased Self-Esteem

Improved Physical Health Resilience to Life's Challenges.

OUT COME #1 ENHANCED RELATIONSHIPS

The journey of growing up involves a lot of changes, and one of the most exciting parts is learning more about who you are. As you become more self-aware—getting to know your feelings, what sets them off, thinking about your actions, staying present, and asking others for their thoughts—you start to see some pretty cool changes in your life, especially in how you connect with people. Let's dive into how this deeper understanding of yourself leads to better relationships with friends, family, and even new people you meet.

WHAT DOES STRONGER SELF-AWARENESS LOOK LIKE?

Imagine you're the captain of a ship. Self-awareness is your map and compass combined. It helps you know where you are, where you're heading, and how to navigate through rough waters. Recognizing your emotions is like checking the weather; understanding your triggers is like knowing where the storms are; reflecting on your actions is like plotting your course; practicing mindfulness is like steering the ship smoothly, and seeking feedback is like listening to your crew's advice to avoid hidden rocks.

HOW DOES THIS LEAD TO ENHANCED RELATIONSHIPS?

Better Communication

When you understand your feelings and where they come from, you can explain them better to others. It's like if you were upset because you lost a game, instead of just getting angry, you could say, "I'm really disappointed because I worked hard and still lost." This helps others understand you better and can prevent misunderstandings.

Deeper Empathy

Self-awareness isn't just about knowing yourself; it's also about understanding others. It's easier to see why someone else might be upset or happy when you understand why you feel a certain way. It's like if you see someone else lose a game and get upset, you remember how that feels, and instead of thinking they're just a sore loser, you might offer some kind words or support.

Fewer Conflicts

Knowing your triggers helps you stay calm in situations that might have made you explode before. For example, if you know you get really annoyed when someone interrupts you, the next time it happens, instead of yelling, you might take a deep breath and kindly ask them to let you finish. This can stop arguments before they start.

Stronger Friendships

Being self-aware helps you be a better friend. You're more in tune with your friends' feelings and can be there for them when they need you. It's like if your friend is having a bad day, you might notice the small signs (like them being quieterthan usual), and ask them what's wrong. This shows themyou care.

More Authentic Connections

The more you understand yourself, the more confidently you can share your true self with others. This honesty attractspeople because they see you're genuine. It's like if you'rereally into drawing but were nervous people would think it's nerdy. When you embrace that part of you and share your art,you might find others who love it too, or who admire your talent and confidence.

Improved Problem-Solving

When problems do arise, self-awareness helps you handlethem better. You're more likely to think things through and consider how your actions affect others. It's like if you and a friend are arguing over which movie to watch, instead ofinsisting on your choice, you might suggest taking turns choosing, solving the problem while keeping the peace.

Increased Trust

As you become more self-aware and communicate more effectively, people start to trust you more. They know you're honest about your feelings and considerate of theirs. Thistrust is like a strong rope that holds relationships together, even when things get tough.

BRINGING IT ALL TOGETHER

Enhanced relationships are like a beautiful garden that you and your friends and family grow together. Self-awareness is the water and sunlight that help it flourish. You'll have misunderstandings and disagreements because that's part of being human. But with a strong understanding of yourself, you'll be equipped to navigate these challenges more grace- fully, making your relationships stronger and more meaningful.

By developing self-awareness, you're not just improving your own life; you're also making the world around you a little brighter, one relationship at a time. It's a journey worth taking, filled with learning, growth, and deeper connections with the people you care about.most.

OUTCOME #2: ACADEMIC AND PROFESSIONAL SUCCESS

Becoming more self-aware is like unlocking a secret level in a video game that gives you special skills to tackle all sorts of challenges. This isn't just about being better at understanding your feelings or knowing what makes you tick. It's like equipping yourself with a super-powered backpack that helps you climb higher in school and soar in your current or future career. Let's dive into how this magical backpack of self-awareness can lead you to academic and professional success.

SUPERPOWER #1: LASER-FOCUSED CONCENTRATION

Imagine your brain is like a superhero that can focus its powers exactly where it's needed. When you practice mind- fulness and meditation, it's like training your brain to concen- trate on your homework, projects, or studying for that big test without getting distracted every five seconds by a text message or a new video game level. This means you get your work done better and faster, leading to better grades and more time for fun.

SUPERPOWER #2: THE SHIELD OF STRESS-RESISTANCE

School and work can sometimes feel like facing a giant monster in a game. Tests, deadlines, presentations – they can all pile up, making you feel overwhelmed. Being self-aware helps you recognize when you're starting to feel stressed and manage those feelings before they turn into a full-blown monster attack. Maybe you realize that taking deep breaths or a short walk helps calm you down. With this shield, stress doesn't knock you down; you keep moving forward, calm, and ready to tackle any challenge.

SUPERPOWER #3: THE COMPASS OF GOAL-SETTING

Knowing yourself means knowing what you're good at and what you enjoy. It's like having a compass that points you in the direction of your dreams. Maybe you discover you have aknack for storytelling, so you aim for a future as a writer. Or perhaps you realize you love helping people and set your sights on becoming a nurse. With this compass, you can set goals for your studies and future career that truly match who you are and what you love, making the journey more excitingand rewarding.

SUPERPOWER #4: THE COMMUNICATOR

Ever watch superheroes who can talk to anyone, from aliens to animals? That's what becoming more self-aware can do for your communication skills. When you understand your emotions and how to express them, you become better at talking with teachers, classmates, and later, colleagues and bosses. You know how to ask for help when you need it, share your ideas confidently, and listen to others. This super- power helps you build strong relationships that can support you through school and kickstart your career.

SUPERPOWER #5: THE PROBLEM-SOLVER

Self-awareness is like having a tool belt with just the right gadget for any problem. When you reflect on your actions and seek feedback, you learn from both successes and mistakes. This means you get really good at figuring out solu- tions to tricky homework problems or finding creative ways to complete a group project. And in the professional world, being a problem-solver can make you stand out as someone who's not only smart but also adaptable and innovative.

SUPERPOWER #6: THE RESILIENCE BOOSTER

Life is full of ups and downs, like a roller coaster with thrilling highs and scary drops. Developing stronger self- awareness gives you the resilience to handle this ride. You learn that failure isn't the end of the world but a chance to grow. Didn't ace that test? You'll study differently next time. The project didn't turn out as planned? You'll gather feedback and improve. This resilience means you bounce back faster and stronger, ready for the next challenge in school and beyond.

SUPERPOWER #7: THE NETWORKER

Finally, self-awareness helps you become a master networker. By seeking feedback and understanding your emotions, you show others that you value their opinions and care aboutimproving yourself. This draws people to you, helping you build a network of friends, mentors, and, eventually, profes- sional connections. These are the folks who will cheer you on,offer advice, and might even open doors to exciting opportu- nities in your future career.

PUTTING IT ALL TOGETHER

So, there you have it. Developing stronger self-awareness isn't just about getting to know yourself better; it's about unlocking these superpowers that lead to academic and professional success. Like any superhero in training, it takes practice, patience, and a bit of trial and error. But the rewards are worth it. With these powers in your backpack, you're not just preparing for tests and assignments; you're setting the stage for a bright, successful future in whatever path you choose to follow.

Remember, every superhero has a unique journey. Your path to academic and professional success will be your own, filled with personal victories, learning moments, and, most impor- tantly, the joy of discovering just how much you can achieve. So, keep exploring, keep learning about yourself, and get ready to soar. The world is waiting for your superpowers to shine.

OUTCOME #3: BETTER DECISION MAKING

Imagine you're the hero of your own video game. In this game, every level you conquer, puzzle you solve, or enemy you defeat is based on your decisions. Now, what if I told you that leveling up your self-awareness is like unlocking a secret power-up that makes your in-game choices smarter, quicker, and more likely to lead to victory? That's what we're talking about when we link stronger self-aware- ness to better decision-making. Let's dive into how this works, step by step.

UNDERSTANDING YOUR EMOTIONAL DASHBOARD

First up, imagine your emotions are like a dashboard in a car, with lights and gauges telling you what's going on under the hood. When you recognize your emotions, it's like under- standing what each light and gauge means. If the "anger" light goes on, maybe it's because someone cut you off (in life, not just in traffic). Knowing this helps you decide how to react without overheating the engine.

NAVIGATING YOUR EMOTIONAL MAP

Understanding your triggers is like having a GPS that warns you about roadblocks or traffic jams ahead. If you know certain situations make you anxious or upset (like speaking infront of the class), you can prepare better. Maybe you'll take a different route by practicing more or finding strategies to calm down, leading to a smoother journey.

REFLECTING ON YOUR JOURNEY

Reflecting on past decisions is like looking in your rearview mirror. It helps you see what's behind you — the good moves you made and the times you might have taken a wrong turn. This hindsight is super valuable because it guides your future choices, ensuring you don't make the same mistakes twice.

PRACTICING MINDFULNESS: THE ART OF DRIVING IN THE MOMENT

Mindfulness is all about being in the now, like focusing on the road while you drive. It's easy to get distracted by what happened at school yesterday or what you're going to do after homework, but staying in the present helps you make better choices. It's like not texting while driving; keeping your attention on what's happening right now ensures you don't miss important cues or opportunities.

SEEKING FEEDBACK: ASKING FOR DIRECTIONS

Sometimes, even the best drivers need to ask for directions. Seeking feedback is just that — asking teachers, friends, or family for their thoughts on your choices. Maybe they've driven this way before and can tell you about a shortcut you didn't know or warn you about a pothole in the road. Their insights can help you make better decisions moving forward.

MAKING BETTER DECISIONS: THE DESTINATION

With all these tools — recognizing your emotions, understanding your triggers, reflecting on past decisions, practicing mindfulness, and seeking feedback — you're set up for success. Making better decisions becomes easier because you have a clearer map of where you are, where you want to go, and the best way to get there.

CHOOSING YOUR PATH

Now, with every choice you face, from deciding to study now

or watch TV, to choosing who you spend time with, you're better equipped. You can ask yourself, "How do I feel about this? What happened last time I was in a similar situation? Am I paying attention to what's happening right now? What do my trusted co-pilots (friends, family) think?"

REACHING YOUR GOALS

Every good decision you make is like completing another level in your game. Whether it's acing a test because you chose to study or maintaining a great friendship because you decided to talk things out instead of getting angry, these deci- sions add up. They lead you closer to your goals, whether that's getting into a good college, landing your dream job, or just being happy and healthy.

CONCLUSION: LEVELING UP

Becoming more self-aware and making better decisions because of it is like leveling up in real life. It's about knowing yourself, navigating challenges more smartly, and reaching your goals more efficiently. And just like in video games, there will be times you need to pause, assess the situation, and maybe even consult the guidebook (or, in real life, ask for advice). But every decision, and every step forward, makes you more skilled, more confident, and ready for whatever comes next on your journey. So, keep leveling up your self-awareness, and watch how your decision-making skills transform your life's game into an epic adventure. With each choice, you're not just moving forward; you're crafting a story of success, resilience, and happiness that's uniquely yours.

OUTCOME #4: INCREASED SELF ESTEEM

Embarking on the journey of self-awareness is akin to setting sail on an expedition of self-discovery, with the compass of introspection guiding the way. This voyage, chal- lenging yet enriching, paves the path to a treasure often sought but hard to find: increased self-esteem. Let's navigate through how cultivating a deeper sense of self-awareness acts as the cornerstone for building a resilient and flourishing sense of self-worth.

UNRAVELING THE LAYERS OF SELF-AWARENESS

At the heart of self-awareness lies the capacity to recognize and understand one's emotions, to pinpoint triggers that sway the emotional compass, and to reflect upon past experi- ences with a critical yet compassionate eye. This process is further enriched through the practices of mindfulness and meditation, alongside the invaluable insights gained from seeking feedback. Like an artist becoming intimate with every stroke of the brush, this introspective journey allows young adults to become the architects of their own psyche, under- standing the depth of their emotions, the contours of their triggers, and the shades of their character.

THE SCAFFOLDING OF SELF-ESTEEM

Self-esteem, in its essence, is the scaffold upon which we build our perception of our worth and capabilities. It is not a static monument but a dynamic structure that evolves with every experience, every reflection, and every piece of feed- back we integrate into our understanding of ourselves. Through the lens of heightened self-awareness, this scaf- folding becomes not just more robust but also more intricate, reflecting a truer representation of who we are.

THE ROLE OF EMOTIONAL RECOGNITION

Recognizing our emotions is akin to reading the signs along the journey of life. By understanding the language of our feel-ings, we empower ourselves to respond rather than react. This empowerment stems from a place of knowledge, where emotions are neither enemies nor tyrants but messengers that guide us through our internal landscape. The ability to iden- tify and articulate these emotions lays the groundwork for a self-esteem that is both informed and resilient, standing firm in the face of life's tempests.

UNDERSTANDING TRIGGERS AND REFLECTION

Knowing what triggers our emotions is like mapping the terrain of our internal world. It allows us to anticipate, prepare for, and navigate through the emotional landscapes that might otherwise destabilize us. Coupled with the habit of reflection, this awareness fosters a deeper understanding of our patterns and behaviors. It's through this reflective prac- tice that we learn not only to avoid certain pitfalls but also to recognize our growth and strengths, fueling a sense of achievement and bolstering our self-esteem.

MINDFULNESS, MEDITATION, AND FEEDBACK

Mindfulness and meditation serve as the anchors that keep us grounded in the present, enabling us to engage with our experiences from a place of balance and clarity. This present- centered awareness sharpens our focus, calms our minds, and opens our hearts, creating a fertile ground for self-compassion and self-acceptance. Similarly, seeking and processing feedback is akin to looking into mirrors held up by those around us. These reflections, varied and multifaceted, provide perspectives outside our own, challenging our self- perception and encouraging growth. Through these practices, we learn to value ourselves not just for our achievements but for our efforts and intentions, thus enhancing our self-esteem.

THE TRANSFORMATION: INCREASED SELF-ESTEEM

The transformation wrought by enhanced self-awareness is profound. With each step on this journey, the layers of self- doubt and insecurity are peeled away, revealing a core of self-assurance and worth. This increased self-esteem is not a loud proclamation for the world to hear but a quiet certainty that resonates within, informing our choices, our relationships, and our view of the world.

CONFIDENCE IN DECISION-MAKING

Armed with an understanding of their emotions and triggers, and honed by reflection, individuals stand on firmer ground when making decisions. This confidence is not born out of arrogance but out of a clear understanding of one's values, desires, and boundaries. It reflects a trust in one's ability to navigate the complexities of life, making choices that align with one's true self.

RESILIENCE IN THE FACE OF CHALLENGES

Increased self-esteem fosters resilience, enabling individuals to face challenges not as insurmountable obstacles but as opportunities for growth. This resilience is the shield that guards against the arrows of criticism and failure, allowing one to emerge from trials not diminished but strengthened, with a renewed sense of capability and endurance.

AUTHENTIC RELATIONSHIPS

With a foundation of strong self-esteem, relationships transform into arenas of authenticity and depth. Understanding oneself paves the way for understanding others, fostering connections that are rooted in empathy, respect, and genuine affection. It's through these authentic interactions that self- esteem finds both affirmation and expression, in a cycle of mutual growth and appreciation.

CONCLUSION: THE ENDLESS HORIZON

The journey of self-awareness, with its promise of increased self-esteem, is not a destination but an ongoing adventure. It's a voyage that demands courage to face the unknown territo- ries within us, resilience to weather the storms of doubt and criticism, and openness to embrace the myriad reflections of who we are. This journey, intricate and uniquely personal, holds the key to unlocking the treasure of self-esteem, a trea- sure that, once found, illuminates every aspect of our lives with its glow.

In the end, the quest for self-awareness and the increased self-esteem that follows is about coming home to oneself, recog- nizing and embracing the full spectrum of who we are. It's about standing firmly within ourselves, not in isolation but in rich connection with the world around us, empowered by the deep, unshakeable knowledge of our worth.

OUTCOME #:5 IMPROVED PHYSICAL HEALTH

Enhancing your physical health is like upgrading your smartphone to the latest model—the performance improves, it handles tasks better, and overall, it just feels good to use. When you put in the effort to boost your phys- ical health, you unlock a bunch of cool benefits that affect not just how you move and feel but also how you think and interact with the world. Let's check out at least five awesome outcomes of getting your health on a winning streak.

1. BOOSTED ENERGY LEVELS

Imagine waking up feeling like you've got a full battery, ready to tackle whatever the day throws at you. That's what enhanced physical health can do. Instead of dragging your- self through the day, running on low power, improving your fitness can crank up your energy levels. It's like having an extra tank of gas; you can go longer and do more without hitting that dreaded afternoon slump. More energy means you're all set to crush it at school, hit the gym, or hang out with friends without feeling like a zombie.

2. SHARPER MIND

Getting your body in shape is like giving your brain a super-charge. Regular exercise pumps more blood to your brain, which is kind of like watering a plant—it helps it grow and function better. This leads to improved concentration, sharper memory, and better problem-solving skills. So, not only does your body benefit, but your grades might see a boost, too, because you're able to focus better and remember things more clearly. It's like unlocking a new level in your favorite game where you suddenly have all these extra skills and abilities.

3. STRONGER IMMUNE SYSTEM

Ever wish you had a shield that could protect you from getting sick? Enhancing your physical health can do that. Regular exercise and a healthy diet strengthen your immune system, making it better at fighting off bugs and viruses. This means you're less likely to catch that cold going around school or be knocked down by the flu. It's like having an antivirus on your computer; you're less vulnerable to threats and can keep running smoothly without annoying inter- ruptions.

4. IMPROVED MOOD

Boosting your physical health can turn you into a positivity powerhouse. Exercise releases endorphins, which are chemi- cals in your brain that act like natural painkillers and mood lifters. Think of them as the body's happy pills. This can lead to feeling more upbeat, less stressed, and more relaxed. It's like the sun coming out after a bunch of rainy days; every- thing just feels brighter and better. So, on top of looking great, you're also in a better mood,

139

which makes hanging out with you even more awesome.

1. BETTER SLEEP

Last but definitely not least, working on your physical health can score you some quality zzz's. When you're active during the day, your body is more ready to rest at night, leading to deeper and more restful sleep. It's like following the perfect recipe for a delicious meal; do the right steps, and you get amazing results. Better sleep means you wake up feeling refreshed and ready to go, instead of hitting snooze a dozen times. Plus, good sleep is crucial for growth, brain develop- ment, and keeping your mood stable.

2. INCREASED LONGEVITY AND QUALITY OF LIFE

Lastly, enhancing your physical health is an investment in your future, much like saving money for retirement. By taking care of your body now, you're setting yourself up for a longer, more enjoyable life. Regular physical activity and healthy eating habits can reduce the risk of chronic diseases such as heart disease, diabetes, and obesity. This means more years to enjoy the things you love, from traveling and exploring to spending time with loved ones. It's about addinglife to your years, not just years to your life, ensuring thateach day is lived to the fullest.

CONCLUSION

Stepping up your physical health game is a win-win. You look good, feel good, and even think better. It's like a magic formula for being your best self. Whether it's having more energy, a sharper mind, a stronger defense against sickness, a sunnier outlook on life, or just snoozing better at night, the benefits are too good to pass up. So, lace up those sneakers, grab a water bottle, and get moving—your body (and brain) will thank you!

OUTCOME #: 6 RESILENCE TO LIFE CHALLENGES

In the grand tapestry of life, resilience stands as a testament to our ability to face challenges head-on, learn from them, and emerge stronger. This remarkable capacity to withstand life's storms is not just a trait of the fortunate few but a skill that can be nurtured and developed, particularly through the lens of increased self-awareness. Let's explore how this deepened understanding of oneself cultivates resilience, equipping young adults with the armor they need to brave the battles of life.

THE FOUNDATION OF RESILIENCE

Resilience is often likened to a tree that bends in the storm but doesn't break. The roots of this tree are self-awareness — the profound understanding of our emotions, triggers, thoughts, and behaviors. Just as a tree draws nourishment from the soil, resilience is fueled by our insights into ourpsyche, enabling us to stand tall amidst adversity.

RECOGNIZING EMOTIONS: THE FIRST LINE OF DEFENSE

Understanding our emotions is akin to identifying the winds that sway us. By recognizing these feelings, we learn not to be overpowered by them but to ride them like waves. This awareness allows us to approach situations with a clarity that prevents us from being swept away by emotional turbulence, laying the groundwork for resilient action.

UNDERSTANDING TRIGGERS: MAPPING THE BATTLEFIELD

Knowledge of what triggers our emotional responses is like having a map of the battlefield before the fight begins. This insight gives us foresight and preparation. Instead of being ambushed by unexpected emotional reactions, we can strate- gize and fortify our defenses, ensuring that we remain composed and deliberate in our actions.

REFLECTION: LEARNING FROM PAST BATTLES

The act of reflecting on our past — thinking back on how we've handled previous challenges — serves as a debriefing session. It's a time to assess which strategies worked, which didn't, and why. This process of continuous learning and adaptation is at the heart of resilience. It ensures that with each challenge faced, we grow wiser, stronger, and more prepared for the next.

MINDFULNESS AND MEDITATION: STRENGTHENING THE INNER FORTRESS

Mindfulness and meditation are the practices that strengthen our inner fortress. They teach us to remain present and calm, even in the heat of battle. By exercising mindfulness, we learn to detach from the chaos of the moment and view our circum-stances with a balanced perspective. This equanimity is a powerful ally in maintaining our resolve and composure, essential traits of the resilient spirit.

SEEKING FEEDBACK: ALLIES IN THE STRUGGLE

No warrior fights alone, and in the journey toward resilience, feedback from others serves as the counsel of trusted allies. Seeking and reflecting on the perspectives of friends, family, and mentors helps us see blind spots in our armor, offering opportunities for growth and strengthening. It's through this openness to feedback that we can fortify our resilience, knowing that we are supported and that our strategies are sound.

STRENGTHENING RELATIONSHIPS THROUGH EMPATHY

The journey of self-awareness not only fosters resilience within but also enhances our ability to connect with others. By understanding our own emotions and triggers, wedevelop empathy, recognizing that others face their battles too. This empathy strengthens our relationships, providing a support network that further bolsters our resilience.

THE MANIFESTATION OF RESILIENCE

With the foundation of self-awareness firmly in place,resilience manifests in several key areas of a young adult'slife:

1)   Facing Failure with Fortitude

The resilient individual sees failure not as a defeat but as a lesson. Armed with self-awareness, they can analyze their emotions and reactions to failure, learn from the experience, and apply these lessons moving forward. This attitude trans-forms obstacles into stepping stones, fostering a growth mindset that is central to resilience.

2)   Adapting to Change with Agility

Change is an inevitable part of life, often bringing uncertainty and discomfort. However, for those who have cultivated resilience through self-awareness, change is met with agility and openness. Understanding their internal landscape allows them to navigate the external shifts with confidence, adaptingtheir thoughts and behaviors to align with new realities.

3) Maintaining Hope in Adversity

Resilience is deeply intertwined with hope — the belief that no matter how tough the situation is, there is a path forward. This hope is not naive but grounded in the self-aware indi- vidual's knowledge of their strengths and capacities. It's a hope that's informed by past victories, no matter how small, and the understanding that challenges are temporary and surmountable.

CONCLUSION: THE RESILIENT JOURNEY

The path to resilience, paved with the stones of self-aware- ness, is a journey of continuous growth and learning. It's about recognizing our emotions and triggers, reflecting on our experiences, staying present through mindfulness, and embracing the wisdom found in feedback. This journey equips young adults with the tools to face life's challenges not just with hope but with confidence in their ability to overcome.

Resilience, therefore, is not an inherent trait but a skill honed through the deliberate practice of self-awareness. It's a testa- ment to the strength that lies within each of us, waiting to be unleashed. As young adults embark on this journey, they do so knowing that each step taken in self-awareness is a step toward becoming the master of their fate, capable of weath- ering any storm and thriving in the aftermath.

CONCLUSION

As we navigate through the intricate journey of life, the cultivation of stronger self-awareness through emotional regulation emerges as a beacon, guiding us toward a multi- tude of desirable outcomes. These six outcomes—enhanced relationships, academic and professional success, better deci- sion-making, increased self-esteem, improved physical health, and resilience to life's challenges—are not mere desti- nations but milestones along the path of personal growth and fulfillment. Let's take a moment to reflect on how these outcomes intertwine, each a thread in the tapestry of a well- lived life.

Enhanced Relationships: The foundation of strong self-awareness is the bedrock upon which we build deeper, more meaningful connections with others. By understanding our emotions and triggers, we foster empathy and compassion, not just for ourselves but for those around us. This empathy allows us to communicate more effectively, to listen actively, and to engage in relationships with authenticity and depth.

As we navigate the complexities of human interaction with greater awareness, we cultivate bonds that are both enriching and supportive, providing a network of companionship and understanding that enriches every aspect of our lives.

Academic and Professional Success: The journey towards

self-awareness equips us with the tools necessary for achieving our goals in the classroom and beyond. By recog- nizing our strengths and areas for growth, we can tailor our learning strategies and career paths to align with our true selves. This alignment not only enhances our capacity forsuccess but also ensures that our achievements are deeply fulfilling, resonating with our core values and aspirations.

Better Decision Making: With the compass of self-awareness in hand, we navigate the sea of choices with greater confi- dence and clarity. Understanding our emotional responsesand the triggers that elicit them allows us to approach deci- sions with a balanced perspective, considering not only the immediate impact but also the long-term implications of our actions. This thoughtful approach to decision-making ensuresthat our choices reflect our true intentions and lead us closer to the lives we wish to lead.

Increased Self-Esteem: At the heart of self-awareness lies the key to unlocking our self-esteem. By embracing our authentic selves, acknowledging our achievements, and learning from our setbacks, we cultivate a sense of self-worth that is both resilient and expansive. This self-esteem acts as a shield against the slings and arrows of external criticism and as a wellspring of motivation and courage, empowering us to pursue our dreams with tenacity and grace.

Improved Physical Health: Equally important, enhancing our physical health is a direct benefit of stronger self-aware- ness. As we become more attuned to our bodies' needs and signals, we're better positioned to make choices that promote physical well-being. Regular exercise, balanced nutrition, and adequate rest are all decisions influenced by our self-aware- ness. This focus on physical health is not just about avoiding illness; it's about thriving. It's the difference between barely charging your phone to get through the day and keeping it fully powered so you're ready for anything. With improved physical health, we experience fewer limitations, enjoy more vitality, and can engage more fully in all areas of life, from personal pursuits to academic and professional endeavors.

Resilience to Life's Challenges: Perhaps the most profound outcome of stronger self-awareness is the resilience it fosters. Equipped with a deep understanding of ourselves, we face life's inevitable challenges not as insurmountable obstacles but as opportunities for growth. This resilience enables us to weather the storms of adversity, to adapt to changing circum-stances, and to emerge from each trial with greater wisdom and strength.

In conclusion, the pursuit of stronger emotional regulation and self-awareness is a noble and rewarding endeavor, one that yields rich dividends across the spectrum of human experience. From the quality of our relationships to the achievements of our careers, from the wisdom of our deci- sions to the strength of our self-esteem and resilience, self- awareness is the thread that weaves together the fabric of a fulfilling life. As we continue on this journey, let us cherish each step, knowing that with greater self-awareness comes the power to shape our destinies with intention, grace, and courage.

REFERENCES

Books and Workbooks

- McKay, M., Wood, J. C., & Brantley, J. (2007). *The Dialectical Behavior Therapy Skills Workbook*. New Harbinger Publications.

- Greenberger, D., & Padesky, C. A. (2015). *Mind over mood, second edition: Change how you feel by changing the way you think*. Guilford Press.

- Neff, K. (2011). *Self-Compassion: The Proven Power of Being Kind to Yourself*. William Morrow.

- Leahy, R. L., Tirch, D., & Napolitano, L. A. (2011). *Emotion Regulation in Psychotherapy: A Practitioner's Guide*. Guilford Press.

Research Articles and Journals

- Gross, J. J. (1998). The emerging field of emotion regulation: An integrative review. *Review of General Psychology*, 2(3), 271-299. Kabat-Zinn, J. (2003). Mindfulness-based interventions in context: Past, present, and future. *Clinical Psychology: Science and Practice*, 10(2), 144-156.

Online Resources

- Greater Good in Action (GGIA) - University of California, Berkeley

- A resource hub offering science-based practices for a meaningful life, including specific exercises for emotional regulation, mindfulness, and self-compassion.

- The Center for Mindfulness & Compassion (CMC) - Harvard Medical School

- Provides resources, research findings, and training opportunities related to mindfulness and compassion, with a focus on their applications for improving mental health and well-being.

152 • REFERENCES

Apps

Headspace and Calm

Both apps offer guided meditations, sleep stories, and mindfulness exercises that can help young adults learn to regulate their emotions and manage stress effectively.

Moodnotes

An app designed to track moods and thoughts, helping users identify patterns in their emotional responses and offering strategies for positive change. These references provide a mix of theoretical foundations, prac- tical exercises, and accessible tools for learning about and improving emotional regulation. Incorporating these resources into your book can offer young adults a comprehensive guide to understanding their emotions and learning effective strategies for managing them. Remember to check the latest editions or publications for the most up-to-date information.

For young adults looking to delve deeper into CBT exercises,

Books:

- Greenberger, D., & Padesky, C. A. (2016). *Mind over mood, second edition: Change how you feel by changing the way you think*. Guilford Press.

- Riggenbach, J. (2012). *The CBT Toolbox: A workbook for clients and clinicians*. PESI Publishing.

Websites:

- The Association for Behavioral and Cognitive Therapies (ABCT) website offers resources and information on CBT.

-

Psychology Tools (psychologytools.com) provides CBT worksheets and information.

REFERENCES • 153

Apps:

"CBT Thought Record Diary" and "MoodKit" are apps designed to help users apply CBT techniques in their daily lives. Engaging with these exercises and resources can provide young adults with valuable tools for improving their mental health and emotional regulation. It's important to remember that while self-help resources can be incredibly beneficial, working with a trained therapist can provide personalized guidance and support.

www.ingramcontent.com/pod-product-compliance
Lightning Source LLC
Chambersburg PA
CBHW051525120626
46551CB00012B/1084